Geography Teaching with a Little Latitude

LATITUDE: (now chiefly playful) width: a wide
extent: range: scope: allowance: breadth in
interpretation: extent of signification: freedom from
restraint: laxity: angular distance from the equator
(*geog.*): etc.

(*Chambers Twentieth Century Dictionary*, 1972 edition)

Classroom Close-Ups

A series edited by Gerald Haigh which tries to answer the questions 'what really happens?' and 'what really matters?' in education.

Titles published are:

Classroom Close-Ups: 7

Series Editor: Gerald Haigh

GEOGRAPHY TEACHING WITH A LITTLE LATITUDE

L. J. Jay

Senior Lecturer in Education, University of Sheffield

London
GEORGE ALLEN & UNWIN
Boston   Sydney

First published in 1981

GEORGE ALLEN & UNWIN LTD
40 Museum Street, London WC1A 1LU

© George Allen & Unwin (Publishers) Ltd, 1981

British Library Cataloguing in Publication Data

Jay, Leslie Joseph
  Geography teaching. – (Classroom close-ups; 7).
  1. Geography – Study and teaching – Great Britain
  I. Title   II. Series
  910'.7'1041   G76.5.G7   80-41364

  ISBN 0-04-371077-8
  ISBN 0-04-371078-6 Pbk

Set in 10 on 11 point Times by Red Lion Setters, London and
printed in Great Britain by
Billing and Sons Ltd.Guildford, London and Worcester

Contents

Figures

Acknowledgements

I am grateful to the following for giving me permission to reprint copyright material: The Bodley Head Ltd and A. D. Peters & Co. Ltd for the last verse of 'The Moorland Map' by Ivor Brown, which appeared in his book *Random Words*; W. & R. Chambers Ltd for the definition of 'latitude' from *Chambers Twentieth Century Dictionary*, 1972 edition; Doncaster Metropolitan Borough Council, Notre Dame High School Leeds and Mrs B. Urquhart for Figure 11; Mrs J. F. Lisle of Darling Point, New South Wales, Australia, for the opening verse of 'Romance' by Walter James Turner; Methuen & Co. Ltd for a verse of four lines by A. P. Herbert and a verse of eight lines from G. K. Chesterton's 'Songs of Education II. Geography'; John Murray (Publishers) Ltd for two lines from the poem 'Dorset' by John Betjeman; A. D. Peters & Co. Ltd for two verses, each of eight lines, from *The Weather Eye* by C. R. Benstead; the Royal Meteorological Society for the mnemonic printed on page 230 of *Weather Lore* by Richard Inwards, 1950 edition.

I also wish to thank my wife who gave me invaluable assistance in the preparation of material and made a number of constructive comments; Heather Ayrton for the cartoons which she drew to illustrate my captions; Lewis Spolton and Michael Gibbons, who read the first draft of the book and offered helpful suggestions; lastly, all those pupils, students, teachers and lecturers, past and present, who at some time or other have shared with me the enjoyment of geography.

L. J. J.

Introduction

Nearly all the books that have been written about the teaching of geography possess two characteristics in common: they concentrate on important, fundamental issues and they are written in a serious vein – so serious, in fact, that many of those who teach or who are preparing to teach never bother to read them. Yet there is a lighter side to learning and it is a poor lesson or lecture which does not occasionally digress from the essentials in order to mention unimportant items, while a humorous aside will often aid the comprehension of a complex problem. It is commendable that writers on teaching technique are keen to emphasise basic principles and fundamental facts, but in doing this to the exclusion of minor matters they tend to drift away from the reality of what actually happens in the classroom. This divergence becomes apparent whenever they offer specimen lessons to illustrate the practical application of the concepts they have been expounding, for in these models of procedure every question posed by the teacher is crisply phrased and neatly designed to develop the lesson topic in logical digestible stages, while all the answers purporting to come from pupils are startlingly correct with no slips of the tongue or wasted words. The accuracy and earnestness of the dialogue seem too good to be true and the young teacher who attempts to imitate these model lessons soon despairs of ever finding a class which responds so impeccably. Yet anyone who has observed an experienced teacher in action is impressed by the dexterity with which unexpected answers are treated, misunderstandings clarified, clumsy phrases re-worded and irrelevancies discarded. All of these verbal thrusts and parries are accompanied by supportive comments tailored to the individual pupil – a mild reproof here, a word of praise there, a gentle jest with another, creating a pattern of conversation which in a purposeful yet unforced manner advances the theme of the lesson without losing the attention or interest of the class. Recent investigations by educational sociologists who have made recordings of lessons in school reveal the complexity of the spoken exchanges between teacher and pupils; they also confirm the important part played by humour and the high proportion of trivial and inconsequential matter which enters into classroom discourse.

In this book I have gathered together items and anecdotes accumulated during many years of studying, teaching and examining geography at various levels, in schools and universities, among adult evening classes or with groups of servicemen, chiefly in Britain but with one year spent in Australia and another in North America. Technical profundities have been avoided as far as possible and footnotes are omitted although sources mentioned in the text are listed at the end of each chapter. The book has been written during moments of relaxation between more serious commitments in geography and education; hopefully the enjoyment I have derived from this exercise will be shared by the reader.

L. J. Jay
Sheffield, 1979

Chapter 1

The Fascination of Place-Names

Many people still retain a firm belief that geography is largely concerned with knowing the location of places. This idea dates back to the time when long-distance travel was both difficult and expensive. People who could read were hungry for the accounts of travellers in remote regions and it was understandable that the journals of explorers were filled with the names of places which they had visited or discovered. Geography and travel were linked in the minds of educated men and their keen interest in this subject was displayed on the shelves of their private libraries which contained many volumes describing the journeys of intrepid wanderers over land and sea. Today, however, few large areas of our world remain unexplored and geography has advanced beyond the elementary stage of location and description to become a scientific discipline which is more satisfying intellectually. Nevertheless, these advances are familiar to a comparatively small number of professionals, and the old idea persists, even among many educated people, that anyone claiming to be a geographer ought to be a human gazetteer, capable of giving a precise location of any place, however small, which crops up in conversation, print or sound broadcast. Thus a recent issue of the *Telegraph Sunday Magazine* carried an advertisement in colour showing a handsome, smiling man in his early thirties wearing a smartly tailored fawn suit of impeccable cut. He holds a pen in one hand while the other rests lightly on a pedestal globe which is turned to reveal the countries of the Middle East. An attractive young woman student is gazing up admiringly at him from her seat alongside the globe. The caption to the picture reads:

'Roy Jones can pinpoint Qal'ap Saura . . . and Umm Wajid and Mahd Dhahah as well. He should do – he lectures in geography. Roy buys his clothes from —— and he rapidly pinpointed this suit as his choice from our summer collection.'

The popularity of quiz programmes on radio and television such as *University Challenge* and *Mastermind*, in which brief factual answers are required to a wide range of questions of general or special knowledge, perpetuates the belief of many listeners that the acquisition of facts which can be conveyed in a short sentence or even a single word remains the substance of specialist subjects which have been studied in depth. This is particularly true of the programme *Mastermind* where contestants are tested not only on their general knowledge but on a specialist topic of their own choosing, for invariably the questions put to a competitor who offers a geographical theme as his specialism are strongly weighted towards recalling the names of physical features, places or economic products. One such competitor, whose chosen theme was 'The geography of Spain', was asked to name, as part of his test, 'the second highest peak in Asturias'. Incidentally, in the *final* round of one of these television contests to choose the 'Mastermind' of the year, one of the questions of general knowledge put to a competitor was 'Is the Tropic of Cancer north or south of the Equator?'. Even if we make allowance for the limited scope of investigation permitted to the question-master of a quiz programme in the space of half an hour, it remains true that many professional geographers are irritated by the low standard of the geographical questions that are posed, for this tends to emphasise the gap between the expert and the layman in their respective conceptions of the scope of modern geography. It helps to explain, moreover, why many teachers avoid giving undue prominence to the location of places in their geography lessons, for they still recoil from the limited concept of the subject exhibited by geographers in the nineteenth century, which required children to commit to memory long lists of meaningless names. This is a great pity, for children as well as adults can derive considerable pleasure from toponymics, the study of place-names, and many a lesson can be enlivened by a brief digression to examine the derivation, history or merely the pronunciation of a geographical name.

W. J. Turner conveyed this pleasure in verse-form in his poem 'Romance':

> When I was but thirteen or so
> I went into a golden land,
> Chimborazo, Cotopaxi
> Took me by the hand.

Long before they reach the age of 13, however, most children who have acquired a taste for reading will happily pore over the glossy maps in a brightly coloured atlas or dip into a book of travel and adventure, savouring the exotic names mentioned therein. Zambezi, Chattanooga, Vladivostok, Goondiwindi, Trincomalee – how deliciously they sound when uttered aloud or rolled softly around the tongue! I wonder if a West Indian boy in Jamaica is equally fascinated to read in a book about Basingstoke, Nottingham or Kidderminster? It does not matter if places are subsequently found to be less romantic in reality than their names would suggest, for this is merely one facet of the disillusionment which may accompany growing up; it is the initial attraction of the name which often gives a person his earliest introduction to matters geographical. Not that remote regions have a monopoly of euphonious names, for they can be collected in Britain by any observant traveller who studies the signposts as he moves around the countryside, or examines a map in an armchair by the fireside when the weather discourages outdoor exercise. Leicestershire harbours the evocative sounds of Willoughby Waterleys, Peatling Parva and Barton-in-the-Beans, and many other counties can yield an equally rich harvest of fascinating names.

In the summer of 1974 an unobtrusive announcement in *The Times* informed readers that the vicar of Piddletrenthide with Alton Pancras and Plush was to become priest-in-charge of Buckhorn Weston and Kington Magna. This sparked off a series of letters to the editor during the ensuing weeks on the subject of quaint place-names. Among the favourites of various contributors were such English villages as Toller Pocorum, Wyke Champflower and Claxby Pluckacre, names which must have recalled for many readers of this correspondence the opening lines of John Betjeman's poem 'Dorset':

> Rime Intrinsica, Fontmell Magna, Sturminster Newton
>   and Melbury Bubb,
> Whist upon whist upon whist upon whist drive, in Institute, Legion
>   and Social Club.

This series of letters to *The Times* was concluded by a lady living in Brussels whose favourite from any country was the eructative name of a station on the railway line from Brussels to Louvain, called Erps-Kwerps.

Ivor Brown was once walking over the lonely uplands of northern England where the boundaries of Yorkshire meet those of Cumbria and Durham when he came across Hagworm Hill amid the ruins of roofless farmsteads and abandoned mine-workings. He wondered whether the hagworm was a parasite which infested the intestines of sheep and as he continued his walk he observed how the grim sound of the places on the map matched the forbidding landscape of frustration and dereliction. He put his thoughts into a poem entitled 'The Moorland Map' which he called a rhyme of ruin; the last of the four verses underlines the struggle to wrest a living from a harsh environment:

Our maps are music and they sing the farmers'
Long battle to wring fodder from the fell:
There's Stony Mea and Nettlepost and Sour Nook,
There's Pasture End and Halfpenny, and Farewell.

Oddities abound in every country. In England there are the villages of Upend near Newmarket and Downend close to Newbury; Bottoms to the south of Todmorden and Toppings a few kilometres away on the borders of Bolton; Shut End in the Staffordshire Black Country and Wide Open north of Newcastle-upon-Tyne; Fighting Cocks east of Darlington, Box near Bath and Wallop in Hampshire. The village of Jump, a few kilometres from Barnsley in Yorkshire, has been the inspiration for many stories of this calibre:

Miner, at bus stop:	'Is this bus going to Jump?'
Bus conductor:	'Yes, it is.'
Miner:	'Then keep it on t'ground while I get on it!'

Every region has some local place which has developed humorous associations so that the mere mention of it in company provokes smiles or open laughter, a fact which professional comedians and pantomime dames exploit to the full in their patter. So do the classroom jokers. In one school where I was teaching the geography of the local region, a reference to Ditchford cunningly tucked into his verbal response to my question by a 12-year-old humorist was sufficient to create an outburst of laughter among the rest of the class; it just happened to be the local funny place. Among the comical names which boast a national notoriety one can mention Knotty Ash in Lancashire and Oshkosh in Wisconsin, USA, while two specimens from the Antipodes are Manangatang in Victoria and Wagga Wagga in New South Wales, Australia. Have you a 'Ditchford' in your neighbourhood?

Exceptionally long names are comical but inconvenient, so that if they occur in populated areas they are generally abbreviated for common usage. Thus Woolloomooloo, a suburb of Sydney, Australia, is locally referred to as the 'loo', just as some thousand km farther north along the coast Woolloongabba, a suburb of Brisbane in Queensland with a fine cricket ground on which Test Matches are played, is known affectionately as the 'Gabba' and is designated as such on the destination boards of city buses. The longest place-name in Britain is a village on the island of Anglesey close to the Menai Bridge. The fifty-eight letters of the full name can be seen on picture postcards and on a sign which extends across the wall of two shops and a garage in the village, although the original

He prefers to use that projection for his world maps – after school he coaches the First Fifteen

full name-plate on the local railway station has now been removed to a museum in Penrhyn Castle, on the outskirts of Bangor. On large-scale Ordnance Survey maps only the first twenty letters of the name are quoted, and this is further reduced in common usage to Llanfair PG. There is a story that when the railway station possessed the full name-plate a young traveller alighted from the London train and gazed in silent wonder at the lengthy name. A Welsh porter came up to him and proudly asked 'And what do you think of Llanfairpwllgwyn ... gogogoch?', to which the visitor replied laconically, 'It's hard to say'. In Australia there are two lakes each with an aboriginal name of nineteen letters, Cadibarrawirracanna in South Australia and Lake Mirranpongapongunna in the Simpson Desert. (The volume, if not the name, of these lakes is greatly reduced in size during the dry season.) The longest place-name in the world is reputed to be a Maori village in the southern Hawkes Bay district of North Island, New Zealand, which is eighty-three letters long, but the most appropriate location for polysyllabic monsters of this kind is in the *Guinness Book of Records*.

In the year 1832 the source of the Mississippi River in North

America was discovered by the Rev. William Boutwell and Henry Schoolcraft when they came upon a small lake about 160 km west of Lake Superior, and they decided to give it a more appropriate name than the Indian word Omushkos, which signified 'elk lake'. The Rev. Boutwell made a rough translation of 'true source' into Latin as 'veritas caput', so his companion suggested using the middle syllables of these two words, when joined together, to create a new name for the lake, Itasca. Fifteen years later this coined word was mentioned in Congress as a possible name for the new state about to be created in this region but after lengthy discussion it was decided to call it Minnesota, after a Sioux word for a local river. There is still a county named Itasca, however, as well as the lake itself. Coined names formed by the fusion of two or more existing names sometimes emerge near state boundaries. In northern Mexico, not far from the boundary with California, there is such a town called Mexicali, while a few kilometres north of the same boundary a smaller township has assumed the name of Calexico. On the other side of the continent, immediately to the east of Washington, DC, there is a peninsula lying between Chesapeake and Delaware bays which is administratively divided between the three states of Delaware, Maryland and Virginia, so it has become known as the Delmarva peninsula. (Not Delmarvir, be it noted, for in the United States 'Va' is the accepted abbreviation for Virginia.) Other examples of coined place-names are those derived from the coalescence of personal names. The town of Arvida, on the banks of the Saguenay River in Quebec Province about 300 km from the confluence with the St Lawrence, possesses the largest aluminium smelter in the world, and its name is derived from the first syllables of the names of a pioneer in the aluminium industry, Arthur Vining Davis. In like manner Pietermaritzburg in South Africa commemorates the names of two pioneer Voortrekkers, Pieter Retief and his companion Gerhard Maritz, while the town of Swellendam about 160 km east of Cape Town is a compound made from Governor Swellengrebel and the maiden name of his wife, Engela ten Damme.

Sometimes a place acquires notoriety as being on the remote fringe of the civilised world. Among the ancient Greeks before the time of Christ such a place was the island of Thule, six days sailing north of Britain, discovered by Pytheas of Massilia on his famous Atlantic voyage to Arctic waters. In New South Wales today the expression used by Australians for their 'ultima Thule' is 'back o' Bourke', whereas in Britain the place which for more than a century has become a synonym for outlandishness is Timbuctoo. (I prefer to emphasise the sense of distance in time as well as in space by using the spelling which was current in the nineteenth century rather than the modern version, Timbuktu.) Samuel Wilberforce, Bishop of Winchester and son of the campaigner for the abolition of slavery, wrote the following lines in between more serious literary works:

> If I were a Cassowary
> On the Plains of Timbuctoo
> I would eat a missionary
> Cassock, band and hymn-book too.

The air of romance and legend associated with this city on a bend of the Niger River has outlived its economic importance, for despite the information to the contrary which is still conveyed in some reference books, Timbuctoo is no longer a flourishing focal point for the trans-Saharan traffic of camel-caravans and trucks. The city was at the zenith of its importance during the fifteenth century when it may have had as many as 20,000 inhabitants, but it is now much inferior as a river port to Bamako, 1,100 km upstream.

Just as the philatelist derives pleasure from collecting and studying postage stamps in groups, whether by country or by theme, in addition to the acquisition of specimens which have an individual appeal, so does the toponymist enjoy the study of place-names collectively as well as finding pleasure in the isolated name. In fact some places are significant simply because their names are representative of a group, and it is the distribution of the places with a common characteristic in their names which has an appeal for the geographer. The Angles and Saxons, who entered Britain from the fifth century onwards, have left a lasting impression of the conditions they encountered in the place-name elements which they bestowed, principally upon the lowlands of Britain. During the Dark Ages much of the country was forested, and the early tribes of English who settled here used a variety of words to distinguish grades of woodland. Thus 'hurst' implied a small wooded hill, 'holt' a thicket, 'shaw' or 'grove' a small wood, and some place-names give a clue to the particular species of tree which was prevalent in that area, for example, Elmstead, Oakhanger, Ashton, Hazelden.

'Weald' or 'walde' (resembling the German word *Wald*) referred to forested land, but the cognate word 'wold' implied a slight difference of meaning when applied to the Wolds of Lincolnshire, or the Cotswolds, for these were uplands from which the woods had been cleared. Pioneer settlers had to cut down the forests before they could cultivate in the lowland areas, a fact which accounts for the frequency of the element 'leah', 'ley' or 'leigh' in English place-names, for this indicated a clearing. The river Avon divides the county of Warwickshire into the Felden (fields) or open country to the south, from which the woods had been removed early on in the English settlement, and the Arden or woodland north of the Avon, where forests persisted to a much later date. This historical distinction is not obvious to the modern traveller as he crosses the county, for nearly all the woodland has now been cleared, but it is still apparent in the distribution of place-names containing the element 'leah', 'ley' or 'leigh', for these are much more numerous north of the Avon (Figure 1).

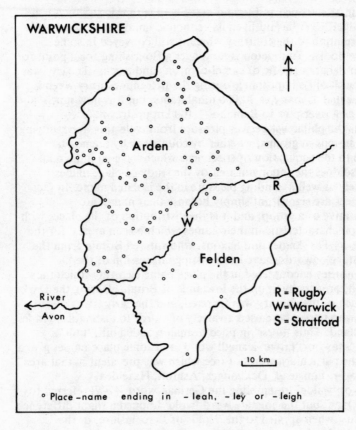

Figure 1 *The former woodlands of Warwickshire*

From the eighth century onwards the Saxons were followed by the Danes who were confined to the area of England north-east of a line from London to Chester after Alfred had made his peace with them, and to this day most of the place-names ending in 'by', a Danish element signifying a farm or dwelling, are located in the area of the old Danelaw, whereas the equivalent Old English ending 'ton' is more common in the south. (The A5 trunk road which cuts across the midland counties broadly coincides with the south-western limits of the Danelaw.) In the north of England Scandinavian invaders added their distinctive elements to place-names, such as 'thwaite' for a clearing and 'garth' for an enclosure or garden. Aysgarth and Bassenthwaite are examples of souvenirs left by the Vikings. What are the predominant place-name elements in your region? Close inspection of the local 1:50,000 Ordnance Survey maps by the class might yield a sizeable crop of Roman, Saxon or Danish specimens, depending on the situation of the school.

The publications of the English Place Name Society provide a wealth of detailed information on this topic. (EPNS means one thing to a jeweller and something else to the keen toponymist!) Two books entitled *The British Isles*, one by G. H. Dury and the other by L. D. Stamp and S. H. Beaver, each have a chapter on the peopling of Britain, while the same theme incorporating examples of the related place-name elements is dealt with in *The New Historical Geography of England* edited by H. C. Darby and *Place Names of the English-Speaking World* written by C. M. Matthews. The relevance of archaeological discoveries to the study of place-names is stressed in Dr Margaret Gelling's book *Signposts to the Past*, which contains a number of interesting maps of place-name elements in England.

The names we bestow give clues to our outlook as well as our origin. The phrases 'Near East' applied to Asia Minor and the Balkan countries, 'Middle East' to the lands bordering the Persian Gulf, and 'Far East' to China and Japan all reflect the viewpoint of an observer in Britain. That which is in the Far East to an Englishman is more accurately in the 'Near North' to an Australian, or in the 'Far West' to the people of California. The Englishman's North Sea is called the Western Ocean (Vesterhavet) by the people of Denmark. Compass direction and physical features are often combined in Chinese place-names; if the component parts are translated they give hints about the appearance of the place. Thus *pei* or *peh* means north or to the north of, *nan* means south, *tung* is east and *si* is west; *kiang*, *ho* or *chwan* mean river, *hu* is a lake, *hai* is sea, *shan* refers to mountains and *king* means a capital city. Combinations of these place-name elements yield Peking and Nanking as the northern and southern capitals respectively; Shantung is the province of the eastern mountains, Shansi the mountainous area to the west. A glance at the relative location of these places will show that the viewpoint is that of an observer in the lowlands of the lower Hwang-ho, which was the nucleus around which the Chinese nation developed. Other provincial names use the same technique: Honan lies south of the Hwang-ho, while Hopei is the province on the northern bank. Hupeh is the province north of the Tung-ting Lake in central China, Hunan is the one to the south of it. One can readily appreciate that the compass was known to the Chinese long before it became familiar to Europeans.

Because the history of invasion and settlement in Britain is of some antiquity, place-names have become modified and distorted over the centuries so that care is needed when interpreting the elements of a name. Shipton was originally a sheep farm and had nothing to do with ships, while Gateshead is probably a modification of goat's head and had no connection with a gate. In the newer lands of America and Australia, on the other hand, where European invasion is comparatively recent, the imprint of successive waves of settlers from a variety of homelands is generally conveyed by the whole name of the place rather than by a prefix or suffix. In the United States of America the place-names are solid reminders of the various nationalities, more particularly the Spanish, Dutch, French and British, who have penetrated and colonised the territory. The Spanish influence spread northwards from Mexico to bestow upon California names such as Los Angeles, San Francisco, Sierra Nevada and the Rio Grande, while in the opposite corner of the country Harlem, Brooklyn, Yonkers and the Bronx recall the former influence of the Dutch in the names of suburbs of the city which was once known as New Amsterdam. French explorers travelled the interior from the mouth of the St Lawrence River to the delta of the Mississippi by way of the Great Lakes. La Salle advanced through the narrows at a place which was anglicised as Detroit, crossed the low portage separating Lake Michigan from headstreams of the Mississippi system and sailed south to reach the Gulf of Mexico. He took possession of this vast drainage basin in the name of King Louis XIV of France, calling it Louisiana. Names of French origin in these interior lowlands include New Orleans, Baton Rouge, St Louis and La Crosse. This influence persisted during the French Revolution, when the American colonists expressed their admiration for Gallic opposition to England by naming many townships with the suffix 'ville', as in Knoxville (Knox was Secretary of War in Washington's Cabinet), Jacksonville (Andrew Jackson fought against the British at New Orleans) and Nashville (General Francis Nash was killed in action against Lord Howe's troops in 1777).

Many of the American names with an Indian origin were established by the French explorers. Ontario is derived from a Huron

Indian word for that lake, Niagara approximates to an Iroquois word for the falls. Michi-guma, meaning 'big water', became Lake Michigan, at the southern end of which wild onions blossomed every summer on a swampy plain between two small streams. In Algonquian language it became known as 'the place of the wild onions'. The French rendered the Algonquian equivalent as Chicagou and in the course of time Americans dropped the final vowel to give it its modern form. Three hundred years ago a Canadian-born Frenchman, Louis Jolliet, and a Jesuit priest, Jacques Marquette, spent one summer travelling along the Mississippi and its tributaries, making friends with the Indians they encountered. Between them they spoke six Indian languages and their explorations enriched the map with a host of names such as Wisconsin, Missouri, Omaha, Kansas, Wabash and Iowa which were all derived from the native American tongues. At one point they heard of a tribe called the Moingouenas, so a nearby stream was named after them. This became abbreviated to La Rivière des Moings, which sounded to other Frenchmen who subsequently travelled this way as if it was called the river of the monks so its spelling was further modified to Rivière des Moines. The city which grew up at the confluence of this river and a tributary called the Raccoon took the name of the main stream and its pronunciation was anglicised to rhyme with 'groyne'.

Before the American colonies achieved independence it was customary to name places after members of the British royal family, with a variety of suffixes. Hence we have Charleston, Williamsburg, Georgia, Annapolis, Carolina, names which were retained after 1776, although during the nineteenth century it became more fashionable to bestow the names of American presidents and politicians on new townships so that within fifty years of independence there were forty Jacksons, thirty Franklins, twenty-three Washingtons, nineteen Lafayettes and eighteen Jeffersons scattered between the Atlantic Ocean and the Mississippi River. Some of these persons lost popularity as the century advanced, but there are now more than a hundred places in the USA rejoicing in the name of Washington, including the federal capital in the east and an entire state in the west. The extension of settlement towards the Pacific resulted in the duplication of many names on both sides of the country as explorers gave the name of their home town to new foundations in the west. Two such men were Amos Lovejoy and Francis Pettygrove who together laid out a township in Oregon at the confluence of the Columbia and Willamette rivers. Amos, who came from Massachusetts, wanted to call the new township Boston, but his companion, a man from Maine, preferred Portland. They tossed a coin to settle the matter and it came down in favour of Portland.

Away from the towns and cities, hundreds of natural features were given names such as Elk Lake, Saddle Mountain, Sweetwater Creek, by trappers, scouts and prospectors. As they moved upstream towards the mountains it was common practice to name branching tributaries East or West Fork, or North and South Fork, a process which could be repeated as the pioneers encountered successive bifurcations of the main channel. Hence the delightfully named West Fork of the South Fork of the North Fork of the San Joaquin River. George R. Stewart has written a book, *Names on the Land*, about the rich variety of American place-names which is fascinating reading.

Both in Australia and in the USA there was extreme sensitivity during the First World War concerning places which had been named by German settlers long before the war began. Several thousand Germans emigrated to Australia in the middle of the nineteenth century and settled in the southern part of the Flinders Range about 32 km east of Adelaide. Many of their townships had German names such as Hahndorf and Lobethal and a flourishing wine industry was begun at Tanundra by a German. Patriotic fervour after 1914 led to the removal of many of these Teutonic place-names from the map. Three towns named Bismarck located in Queensland, South Australia and Tasmania were respectively renamed Maclaglan, Weeroopa and Collins Vale, while Mount Bismarck in Victoria became Mount Kitchener. At the same time American chauvinism resulted in Potsdam in Missouri being changed to Pershing and Brandenburg in Texas became Old Glory. Perhaps the oddest wartime casualty was Germantown in Texas, which was renamed after a local youth who was killed in France on active service; by a strange paradox his name was Schroeder, which strongly suggests a Teutonic origin.

The intense activity of British explorers in opening up colonial possessions overseas during the nineteenth century is reflected in the frequency with which they bestowed the names of Queen Victoria and members of her family upon natural and administrative features. In Canada there is the province of Alberta and the island of Victoria while the capital of Saskatchewan is Regina. In East Africa are Lakes Victoria, Albert and Edward, and Australia has the states of Queensland and Victoria. In the homeland there has been less enthusiasm for naming territories after personages, and the recently created new counties have regional, not personal names. Among the new towns there are Telford in Shropshire, named after the engineer who was at one time official surveyor for that county, and Peterlee in Durham, which perpetuates the name of a former miners' leader.

As a general rule the British seem reluctant to name or rename their towns and cities after national heroes, whose exploits are more modestly commemorated in some street-names on housing estates.

The thoroughfares of most cities and large towns in Britain show an absence of overall planning in layout and nomenclature which makes it extremely difficult for a stranger to find his way about the labyrinth of streets in the city centre. In newer countries overseas, however, the adoption of a gridiron pattern of streets intersecting at right angles divides the buildings of the Central Business District into neat rectangular blocks, thereby providing a basis for easier route-finding by strangers in town, especially if the names can be easily memorised. In the heart of Brisbane in Queensland eight parallel streets named Ann, Adelaide, Queen, Elizabeth, Charlotte, Mary, Margaret and Alice are crossed by William, George, Albert and Edward streets in the loop of the Brisbane River between Central Station and the Botanic Gardens (Figure 2). The *Australian Encyclopaedia* states that these streets are named after various royal personages, although it is difficult to identify these important people with precision.

However, it is not Australia but America which is the country, *par excellence*, of the checkerboard street pattern, for in the USA surveyors followed closely on the heels of explorers, drawing up town-plans and giving names to the streets even before houses had been built along them. Philadelphia in Pennsylvania started the fashion; from the Delaware River westwards to the Schuylkill there is a succession of parallel streets aligned roughly north to south, starting with Front Street and continuing with First and Second on to Thirty-third Street, with other streets, more conventionally named, intersecting them at right angles. Washington, DC, the federal capital, improved on this plan by adding diagonal avenues named after states of the Union, the best known being Pennsylvania Avenue where the President resides. The ultimate in simplicity, however, was the name-pattern adopted by Sacramento, the capital city of California, for its Central Business District. From the Sacramento River on the west, the parallel streets aligned roughly north to south were given numbers, First, Second, Third Street, and so on, while the intersecting streets from the American River on the northern edge of the city, as far as the street called Broadway, were simply designated by the letters of the alphabet. The exception was I Street which became confused so frequently with First Street that it was decided to spell it out as Eye Street! And Eye Street it remains to this day, with the city hall, post office and court house among the important buildings erected upon it (Figure 3).

Investigating the origins of local street-names can be an interesting

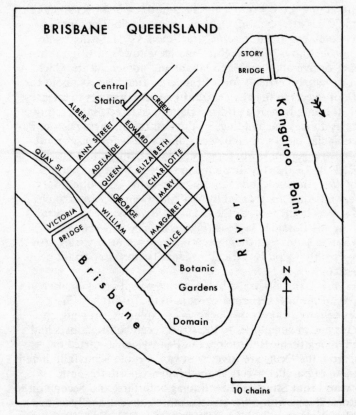

Figure 2: *Street-names in central Brisbane*

exercise for youngsters, whether undertaken as a group or individual activity. Many towns possess a Market Street or Station Road which are self-explanatory; the former is probably older since the market may date from mediaeval or even Saxon times whereas the railway station did not exist before the nineteenth century. Castle Street and Sandpits Lane may refer to features which have long since disappeared from sight, while Northgate or Lydgate Lane possibly refer to the times when the approaches to the town were guarded by a gate in the perimeter walls which was locked at nightfall. A series of adjoining streets which are all named after counties or famous poets may indicate that they were all constructed about the same time in a period of civic expansion of residential suburbs during the nineteenth or present century, while the juxtaposition of Balaclava and Inkerman Streets, named after battles of the Crimean War, gives

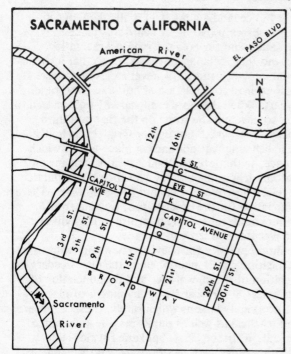

Figure 3: *Street-plan of Sacramento, California*

a clue to their age. Unusual street-names occur in some towns which
need careful elucidation. What is the derivation of the Wicker in
Sheffield, for example, or of Brittox in Devizes, or of Mardol,
Shoplatch and Wyle Cop in the centre of Shrewsbury?

One feature of toponymics which is apt to be neglected is
pronunciation, yet it is characteristic of many places that they are
not necessarily pronounced the way they are spelt. This aspect of
place-names is commonly omitted from textbooks, yet not all of the
names which are printed in books and read by children are spoken
aloud in class. The current fashion for encouraging pupils to search
out information for themselves, whether in group or individual
projects, invariably means that they read much more than is likely to
be talked about in class, so that many names, both of persons and of
places, are literally seen but not heard. One keen young pupil once
startled the assistants in a public library by asking if they had any
books about copper knickers, and when she was asked to explain
more fully she produced a duplicated assignment sheet on a project
which contained a reference to Copernicus.

When I was young I once read a news item in the daily paper concerning Billericay in Essex. I had never heard this place mentioned in conversation and for no valid reason I mentally accented the second and final syllables of the word, so that it rhymed with 'day'. It was a place which somehow never received a mention in formal school lessons or in conversation at home so I forgot all about it for many years. When the word reappeared I was amazed to discover that I ought to have put the stress on the first and third syllables, so that this place rhymed (not inappropriately, I thought) with 'tricky'. The English language abounds in place-names which are tricky to pronounce, so that even well-educated Americans on their first visit to Britain delight the natives with their transatlantic pronunciation of Lye-cess-ter, Wore-wick and Lee-o-min-ster. There are pitfalls in pronunciation for the English, too, ranging from Belvoir in Leicestershire or Beaulieu in Hampshire to Ulgham in Northumberland or Woolfardisworthy in Devon.

It is becoming common practice for television news bulletins to be illustrated by maps locating places mentioned by the news-readers, a distinct aid to recognition of the appearance and pronunciation of tricky names. Nevertheless, a surprisingly large number of places crop up regularly in geography lessons which rarely, if ever, appear in the headlines, and teachers as well as pupils may be uncertain of their correct pronunciation. In the USA, Spokane rhymes with 'man', Butte with 'fruit', while the rivers Potomac and Willamette are stressed on the second syllable. As for Australia, S. J. Baker in his book *The Australian Language* has pointed out the variations in the accented syllable in aboriginal place-names. Some are stressed on the first syllable, as in Canberra, others on the second, for example, Echuca, some stress the third syllable, as in Goondiwindi, while others accent the fourth, for instance Barraganyatti. Sometimes the same word is pronounced differently when it occurs in two states; thus Eungella in Queensland is prounced YUN-gella and accented on the first syllable whereas the town of the same name in New South Wales is pronounced yoon-GELL-a with the stress on the second syllable. Sometimes all syllables are given equal stress, as in the famous Sydney surfing beach on Bondi, pronounced bon-dye, to rhyme with 'sky'. The river Dumaresq in southern Queensland is stressed on the second syllable and pronounced Damerrick, which is about as unfair as any of the four places in England mentioned at the end of the previous paragraph, whose pronunciation is actually Beever, Bewley, Uffam and Woolzerry, all of them stressed on the first syllable. An unorthodox aid to the pronunciation of selected place-names can be rendered in a verse-form which is described in a subsequent chapter.

Although the written language is uniform all over the British Isles there are many different kinds of spoken English, the main dividing line being between the types of standard English and the many varieties of regional dialect. The latter, as A. S. C. Ross has observed in his book *How to Pronounce It*, differ from types of standard English not only in pronunciation and grammar but also in vocabulary, especially in that part which relates to rural matters. Ross has compiled a guide to the pronunciation of 'difficult' words which includes a large selection of geographical place-names; these include Alnwick, Congresbury and Rievaulx in Britain, and Aarhus, Haiti and Srinagar from countries overseas. Many small towns and villages have a local pronunciation which differs from the expected one; BBC news-readers are sometimes unaware of these regional variants, even when they operate from a local radio station. Since many teachers are not natives of the area in which they are working it is often a wise precaution for a newcomer to enlist the help of pupils in compiling a glossary of local place-names which have unexpected pronunciations.

Foreign place-names are as easy to mispronounce as they are to misspell, and those of Poland are probably the most difficult to master. (When coupled with the drastic changes of name which have been effected since the last war, this imposes a double handicap on the study of the geography of Poland.) Of the larger cities Lodz is perhaps the most deceptive, for it looks as if it ought to be pronounced 'Lodds' or 'Loads', although the correct pronunciation approximates to the sound of 'Woodsh'. One is reminded of the comment made by Mark Twain in *The Innocents Abroad* when he was inspecting some drawings by Leonardo da Vinci in the Ambrosian Library, Milan: 'They spell it Vinci and pronounce it Vinchy; foreigners always spell better than they pronounce.'

REFERENCES

S. J. Baker, *The Australian Language* (Sydney, Currawong, 1966).

J. Betjeman, 'Dorset', in *Collected Poems* (London, John Murray, 1958), p. 38.

Ivor Brown, 'The Moorland Map', in *Random Words* (London, Bodley Head, 1971), p. 78.

H. C. Darby (ed.), *A New Historical Geography of England* (Cambridge, Cambridge University Press, 1973).

G. H. Dury, *The British Isles: A Systematic and Regional Geography* (London, Heinemann, 1978), ch. 4.

M. Gelling, *Signposts to the Past: Place-Names and the History of England* (London, Dent, 1978).

C. M. Matthews, *Place Names of the English-Speaking World* (London, Weidenfeld & Nicolson, 1972).

A. S. C. Ross, *How to Pronounce It* (London, Hamish Hamilton, 1970).

L. D. Stamp and S. H. Beaver, *The British Isles* (London, Longman, 1971), ch. 24.

G. R. Stewart, *Names on the Land* (New York, Random House, 1945).

W. J. Turner, 'Romance', in *Selected Poems 1916–1936* (London, Oxford University Press, 1939).

Mark Twain, *The Innocents Abroad* (1869) (New York, Harper, 1929), p. 182.

Chapter 2

Selection à la Carte

Professional geographers may differ in their opinions about the precise nature and scope of their subject, but there has been general agreement among them that maps are fundamental to it. Halford Mackinder once declared that 'in the technique of geography the central fact is the map' and nearly forty years earlier E. C. Bentley had said much the same thing when he differentiated between biography which is about chaps and geography which is about maps.

A map possesses one of two principal functions. On the one hand it can be regarded as a document providing facts about a specific area – its size and shape (if it has clearly marked boundaries), together with the location and extent of selected features within it, such as uplands, rivers, towns, wheatfields, underground mineral deposits or where people live. Viewed from this angle, the map is simply a vehicle for transmitting information, usually by means of symbols, conveying at a glance locations and relationships which might otherwise take many words to describe. Some years ago the town clerk of Sheffield wished to inform the general public that he proposed to order the closure of a narrow iron footbridge which for long had been a right of way over the river Don near to the city centre. Notice of this intention, printed in the columns of the local newspaper, took the form of a single sentence, 620 words long, which provided the precise location of the footbridge. It was presumably essential to publish the notice in legal terminology, but a simple map would have done the job much more succinctly.

The other function of a map is to enable the possessor to find his way across unfamiliar territory. This type, sometimes called a route-map, is an item of the traveller's equipment as vital as his food or clothing. During the school geography course most children encounter maps which have the first of these two functions; in fact, if the subject is badly presented they may come to dislike maps intensely simply because they merely provide more facts which have to be learned and reproduced at examination time. Far fewer pupils, however, become proficient in the practical use of a route-map as a device for finding their way from one place to another – which is a great pity, for it can be the key to much enjoyable recreation in adult life.

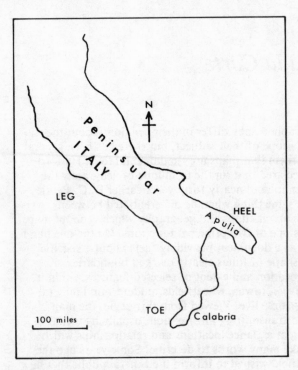

Figure 4: *Leg, heel and toe*

An eminent headmaster of Uppingham School once declared that the geographer thinks in shapes, and most people when looking at the map of a clearly defined area tend to notice first of all its outline which is then compared to some familiar everyday object. 'Italy is a large peninsula, shaped like a trooper's boot and spur' wrote the Rev. R. Turner in his *New and Easy Introduction to Universal Geography* which had reached its tenth edition by the year 1802; and writers today retain the comparison by locating Calabria in the 'toe' and Apulia in the 'heel' of Italy (Figure 4). Another of the Rev. Turner's map-similes was more puzzling, for elsewhere in his book he stated: 'Europe, as to its shape, may be compared to a lady in a sitting posture.' I have turned the map of Europe in all directions in an effort to detect some resemblance to the outline of a seated lady, without much satisfaction! The viewpoint is possibly that of an observer at the southern end of the Ural Mountains, looking westwards. It may have been some grizzled prospector on the Trail of '98 who originally described the narrow coastal strip of Alaska

which stretches south-east from the St Elias Mountains towards
Prince Rupert as a 'panhandle', for the shape of Alaska on a map
resembles an inverted saucepan (Figure 5). The term 'panhandle' is
now applied in America to any long narrow extension of the main
body of territory; Oklahoma has one in its north-western corner,
while its southern neighbour, Texas, not to be outdone, also claims
to have one, centred upon Amarillo, although this is hardly long and
narrow enough to look like a real panhandle.

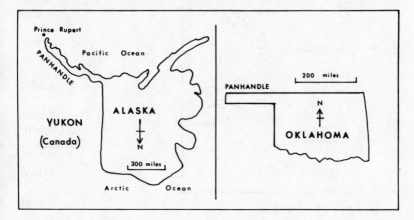

Figure 5: *Panhandles*

The state of Michigan, excluding the Upper Peninsula which lies
north of Lake Michigan, has a shape roughly resembling the outline
of a mitten (for a right hand, palm uppermost, or a left hand, palm
downwards, just as you wish), so that the area north of Detroit
between Lake St Clair and Saginaw Bay represents the thumb (Figure
6). I once saw an advertisement in a Michigan newspaper inserted by
a dealer in ironmongery who claimed that his stock was 'the biggest
in the thumb'.

This tendency to associate the shapes of countries with common
objects was reinforced when children learned much of their
geography from large maps which were hung from hooks on the wall
or draped over an easel. This vertical positioning fostered the idea
that the map was akin to a tapestry or painting hung as if at an
exhibition, and the north direction, which properly should be
indicated by an arm extended parallel to the ground, was more
readily shown by an arm pointing upwards to the ceiling, since on a
wall-map north is 'at the top', Dublin is 'on the right-hand side of
Ireland about halfway down', the river Nile 'flows south and empties

into Lake Victoria' and ships can sail 'around the bottom of Africa'.

Figure 6: *Map of a thumb*

Children are not alone in displaying this wall-map mentality – it is also retained by educated adults. Some years ago, in a book written about Australia for children which was awarded a Book Society prize, the author described the extension of pastoral occupation in Queensland in the following words:

'They overlanded from other States – that means, they moved across country hundreds and hundreds of miles, driving their cattle in front of them and taking their goods on drays and carts. They went past the runs and stations and cattle yards of the men who had come earlier, and they pushed further and further on until they spread right across the top of the map.'

The last five words could have been phrased more felicitously.

A map illustrates the position of selected features fixed at a particular moment of time, although arrows, isochrones and graduated shading can be employed to convey the impression of movement, not only the transfer of commodities and people in space but the growth and decline of crop acreage or human settlement over a period of time. On reflection, a map of population distribution is a very artificial picture of reality, for people are rarely immobile for any length of time: they move about, on foot or in vehicles, sometimes following well-frequented routes along roads or railways, at other times covering the ground in irregular directions. (Contrast for example, the trails blazed in one day by a milk delivery man, a youth on a cycling holiday and the driver of a passenger train.) It is instructive to take into the classroom a shallow box with a glass lid containing a few inches of soil and a colony of ants and allow the children to study for a while the restless movements of the insects, before asking the class to draw a map of the distribution of the ant population contained in the box. Discussion of the difficulty of drawing such a map will serve as a useful introduction to the problems of mapping the distribution of any geographical feature which is capable of movement or removal, whether it concerns people, animals, crops, minerals, vehicles or buildings. Houses are demolished to be replaced by factories or motorways, a field which carries a grain crop one year is pasturing animals the next, an open cast mine becomes exhausted and the surface is planted with trees, and people are always on the move. On this theme there are some interesting exercises for children to do in Book 2 of *New Ways in Geography* by Cole and Beynon, relating to the movement of people within the precincts of the school. See also the article by Bill Pick, 'The school itself as a geographical resource: some ideas', in Volume 5 of *Teaching Geography*, page 25. There is a poster chart which shows the distribution of the world's merchant shipping at a precise moment on a specific date. It shows effectively the concentration of ships in the major ports, the sea-lanes followed by vessels crossing the main oceans and the queue of ships waiting to pass through busy canals. Nevertheless it is like the frame of a moving film which is suddenly stopped by the projectionist – the ships are frozen in their tracks. Hence some of the most effective maps are those on moving film which use the principle of the animated cartoon, so that vivid arrows or layers of colour spread visibly across the map to indicate both the direction and speed of movement of the chosen features.

I once witnessed the drawing of an unusual map when I was in the operations room of an aircraft-carrier moving westwards through the Mediterranean Sea. Towards midnight, as we approached the Strait of Gibraltar, the coastlines of southern Spain and North Africa gradually appeared with increasing clarity on the radar screen, just as if a pair of glow-worms were wriggling their way westwards in a neck-and-neck race. As they moved towards the left-hand side of the screen, trails on the right-hand side became fainter. The two lines on the screen converged westwards and were boldest as we passed through the strait, becoming less sharp as they diverged west of Gibraltar. They finally faded out as the ship moved into the open Atlantic and the shores of Spain and North Africa were left astern, beyond the range of the scanner.

More recently automation and the computer have been applied to the making of maps where the data are already available in digital form such as the agricultural census or the census of population. Sophisticated techniques have greatly speeded up the process of map production and as an example of this method the Department of Geography of the University of Sheffield was able to publish in 1974 a census atlas of South Yorkshire using enumeration district data from the 1971 census, to coincide with the creation of the new administrative unit of South Yorkshire which came into being in April of the same year. In this atlas selected population characteristics of the new county are shown on thirty-five maps drawn to a scale of approximately 1:64,628. The introduction, written by the project director, Bryan Coates, describes the computer techniques which were used to compile the maps.

Inside the geography room many children are introduced to the conventional symbols used on large-scale Ordnance Survey maps, and with practice they become adept at recognising the signs for a slope steeper than 1 in 7 on a major road, or a church with a spire, features which are shown more clearly on the new 1:50,000 series of maps than on the former One-Inch series. Not all of these children, however, will be taken out of doors and shown how to orient a map as a preliminary to finding their way by identifying on the map landmarks seen with their own eyes. Until they do this, many children will never experience the need to hold the map 'upside-down' when they are moving in a southerly direction, unless they are given the task of acting as navigator for one of their parents when travelling in the family car on a long journey. It is a useful exercise in map-reading to supply children with a 1:50,000 OS map, not necessarily of the area around the school, and instruct them to write down the route for a car driver who is travelling south for about 30 km, keeping to MOT class A or B roads, from a given starting point. For pupils who are able to visualise the steepness of roads from the contour patterns, a more testing exercise would be to plan a circular run by bicycle of about 30 km to avoid the steepest hills. Armed with an up-to-date road atlas the brightest in the class could be instructed to describe the succession of roads and right or left turns to be taken by a driver travelling south across a stretch of country from, let us say, Stoney Middleton in Derbyshire to Middleton Stoney in Oxfordshire, using only motorways and A or B class roads. This exercise can be the basis for a game, played in pairs, whereby one pupil plans a cross-country car run and supplies his partner with the road numbers and turnings from a stated starting point, for the solution of the mystery run. The towns and villages passed through en route have to be named in their correct order.

Thank heaven it's Friday! Spot-heights and contours are not the only ways of showing relief

During the war years signposts in the rural areas of Britain were removed by local councils in order to confound any enemy troops who might be dropped into the country by parachute. It was then essential for anyone who went walking in an unfamiliar part of the island to be able to orient his map correctly in order to decide which way to take upon reaching a junction of rural roads. The modern equivalent of finding one's way over strange territory without signposts is offered by the sport of orienteering, which is becoming a popular activity in many schools. Anyone wishing to find out more about this sport should get in touch with officials of the nearest club, the address of which can be obtained from the National Office of the British Orienteering Federation, Lea Green Sports Centre, Matlock, Derbyshire, DE4 5GJ. A useful introduction to the mapwork involved in orienteering, with numerous graded exercises, has been written by John Disley under the title of *Your Way with Map and Compass*. I have noticed that children of 8 to 10 years of age who begin orienteering with their parents soon acquire the ability to orient a map and follow a compass bearing for a measured distance. The minor features of terrain such as knolls, dry ditches and boulders which are marked on the maps specially drawn for orienteering events, along with gradations of colour showing the varied density of undergrowth and forest cover, are learned rapidly when they are encountered in the open air in competitive sport with other children. Moreover the details committed to memory are quickly put to practical use, for the youthful orienteers are rewarded with the thrill of achievement when they arrive at the desired control point, hidden in a hollow in the heart of thickly wooded country, after having followed a chosen bearing for a measured distance, using map and compass.

Although most children are familiar with the appearance of the coloured maps on the glossy pages of a school atlas, and many are able to locate the whereabouts of places by an intelligent use of the gazetteer and reference system of latitude and longitude at the end of the atlas, comparatively few children appreciate the deficiencies of a map of the world or of a large continental mass which result from the impossibility of reproducing accurately the three-dimensional spheroidal earth on a flat two-dimensional atlas map. It is not so long since the phrase 'mathematical geography' implied the study of the properties and construction of the map projections in common use. Paradoxically this application of mathematical concepts has disappeared with the introduction of quantitative geography, and in many secondary schools the characteristics of the main map projections are no longer taught, largely because they are no longer examined. It is not essential for children to make a detailed study of the mathematics involved in map projections, but it is important for them to know in what ways certain atlas maps are incorrect, and this involves some familiarity with the properties of the globe. Any teacher can readily discover whether his pupils possess this fundamental understanding by conducting a simple diagnostic test. The following six questions should be answered individually with the aid of an atlas, and alongside each answer the pupil might add the page numbers of the maps which were used to arrive at that answer. Discussion of suitable replies to the questions when the test has been completed will involve the use of a globe as well as the atlas.

(1) Which is nearest by direct airline to London, England: Cape Town, San Francisco or Singapore?

(2)   If a plane takes the shortest route from Mexico City to London, England, which island in the Atlantic will it fly over?

(3)   Which is larger in area, Alaska or Sudan?

(4)   South America has a different shape on various world maps in the atlas. Which page shows it correctly?

(5)   A plane takes off from an airfield on the Equator at the mouth of the Amazon River in South America and flies on a steady course of north-east (045 degrees by gyro compass). Assuming it can refuel in mid-air without landing, where will its journey end?

(6)   Whereabouts in the world is it possible to make a 6 km journey which involves travelling 2 km due south, then 2 km due east and finally 2 km due north to return to the starting point?

The globe is a neglected item in the equipment of the geography room, often relegated to the top of a store cupboard where it collects a mantle of chalk dust, or if it is the type which is suspended by pulleys from the ceiling the spheroid may become even more oblate as a result of careless handling by pupils. A globe large enough for class demonstration is rather cumbersome to carry around the school, although lighter materials are now being used in their construction which makes them more portable than before. (Not long ago, coinciding but unconnected with a series of terrorist bomb outrages, one educational journal advertised for sale 'an inflatable plastic terrestrial globe, shows all the new countries, can be blown up in half a minute'!)

A globe is essential for demonstrating the properties of and relationship between parallels of latitude, meridians of longitude, Great Circles and lines of constant bearing (rhumb lines), for no atlas map of the world can show all these correctly. Nevertheless, it is possible to appreciate the features which are distorted on a world map without going too deeply into the mathematics of projections. Some years ago W. G. V. Balchin demonstrated the value of identifying those lines of latitude or longitude which are correctly drawn to scale in a map projection (Figure 7). It would be helpful if the publishers of school atlases could indicate in the corner of each map of the world or hemisphere whether it showed areas correctly, or shapes and bearings correctly, or none of these properties. Unfortunately this fundamental information is usually concealed behind a polysyllabic jargon which map-makers love to use, so we read in the small print that one map is drawn on Mollweide's homolographic projection, another uses Lambert's equivalent azimuthal, while a third may be an orthomorphic or conformal projection. We must remember, then, that *homolographic* or *equivalent* refers to an equal-area projection; *orthomorphic*, or *conformal* implies that bearings and the shapes of small features are correctly shown; and *equidistant* signifies that distances are correct along certain lines, usually those radiating from the centre of the map. Some projections do not show any of these features correctly, but by way of compensation they do not exaggerate unduly any of their distortions.

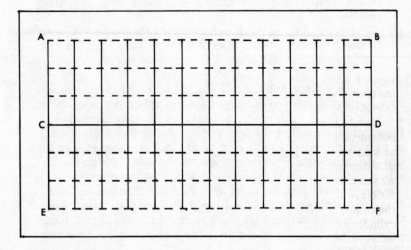

Figure 7: *Simple cylindrical projection or plate carrée. Meridians or parallels which are true to scale are shown by solid lines. C−D represents the Equator, 40,000 km in length.*

Many of the graticules in common use are not true projections in the geometrical sense but have been modified to make them equal-area or orthomorphic, and the well-known Mercator's projection is an example of the latter group. To understand the modifications which are made to obtain the useful properties of Mercator a convenient starting point is the simple cylindrical projection, also known as plate carrée. If the world is represented by a pattern of seventy-two squares, arranged as in Figure 7, the horizontal lines will represent parallels of latitude and the vertical lines will be meridians of longitude, spaced at intervals of thirty degrees. The projection is true to scale along the Equator (C−D) and along each of the meridians, for example, A−C−E, B−D−F, which are half the length of the Equator. However, since the meridians remain equally spaced instead of converging as they approach the Poles, there is

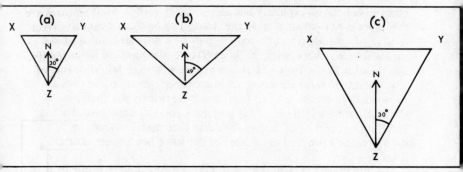

Figure 8 *How the projection affects shape, size and bearing. (a) An imaginary island in latitude 60° north. (b) The same island on the simple cylindrical projection. (c) The same island on Mercator's projection*

considerable distortion of shapes in high latitudes, and the Poles are as long as the Equator. On the globe at latitude 60° the actual length of a degree of longitude is exactly half its length at the Equator, so if we imagine that one of the Shetland Islands (which are in latitude 60°N) is the shape of an equilateral triangle, tapering to a point in the south as in Figure 8a, it will be represented on the simple cylindrical projection by a triangle which is no longer equilateral because the north coastline, X–Y has been 'stretched' to twice its normal length (Figure 8b). Moreover, the bearing of the eastern headland Y, from the southern tip Z of the imaginary island, is considerably in excess of the true bearing of 30° east of north, so that for navigation purposes this projection, although simple to construct, is useless since bearings are not correctly represented. If, however, the plate carrée projection is modified by spacing the lines of latitude farther apart away from the Equator, *in the same proportion as the lines of longitude ought to get closer together*, then around any one point the exaggeration will be equal in all directions, that is, north–south as well as east–west, and this is the property of Mercator's projection. Our imaginary Shetland island will now be shown true to shape but bigger all round (Figure 8c) and, most important of all for navigators, the bearing of the eastern cape Y from the southerly cape Z will be the correct one of 030°.

With the increasing popularity of small boat sailing in the coastal waters around Britain, nautical charts drawn on Mercator's projection are now on sale in many bookshops so that it is not difficult for a teacher to obtain copies of some of these charts for class demonstration, to show that this projection can be used for small areas as well as for a map of the whole world. The scale of the chart is not stated explicitly because it varies with latitude and therefore is not constant over the chart. The navigator uses the fact that 1' of latitude (i.e. one-sixtieth part of a degree) is the length of 1 nautical mile – there being 90 times 60 or 5,400 nautical miles from the Equator to the Pole – so that when he wishes to lay off a run of, say, 8 nautical miles on his chart in a desired direction, he uses a pair of dividers to measure 8' of latitude at the side of the chart, in the approximate latitude of his position, and this measured distance can then be marked off along the desired compass course, for on Mercator's projection all lines of constant bearing are straight lines.

Despite the cumbersome size of a large globe it is desirable to plan a few exercises on it for pupils to conduct individually or in pairs, in order to demonstrate problems of long-distance navigation, atlas maps being inadequate for this purpose. Suppose, for example, we wish to find the shortest route for an airplane to take on a flight from New Orleans on the Gulf of Mexico to Abadan at the head of the Persian Gulf. Both seaports are on the same parallel of latitude, 30° north of the Equator, so if the plane left New Orleans on a constant course due east (090° by gyro compass) it would travel about 11,800 km along this rhumb line to reach Abadan. The Great Circle route between these two ports, however, which can be found by stretching a piece of string over the surface of the globe from New Orleans to Abadan, passes over the Gulf of St Lawrence, Newfoundland, northern Britain and the Black Sea. It is a route which involves frequent changes of course, yet it is 1,300 km shorter than the rhumb line along the parallel of latitude of 30° north. A similar exercise could be conducted to find the shortest air flight from Cape Town in South Africa to Sydney in Australia, for these two ports are roughly on the same line of latitude, but in this case the Great Circle route would bend southwards, close to the Antarctic Circle south of Kerguelen Island.

Before leaving the subject of globe and atlas it might be fitting to add a few comments on the diagnostic test questions given earlier in this chapter. To answer question 1, a piece of string stretched over the surface of a globe between London and each of the three cities in turn will indicate which one is nearest to London and will reveal how inaccurate are most world maps for measuring comparative distances. The same piece of string can be used in question 2 to demonstrate that a plane flying directly from Mexico City to London does not pass over Bermuda or one of the Bahamas, but an island much farther north. A book of reference such as *Whitaker's Almanac* will yield the statistics to settle question 3. There is no decisive answer to the fourth question, since it will depend upon the variety of world maps available in the atlas being used, but the comparison of South America on various atlas maps and the globe should lead to a profitable class discussion. The fifth question provides an opportunity to distinguish between a Great Circle and a rhumb line; in this instance, since the aircraft is steering a constant course, we are dealing with a rhumb line. Hence the plane will not be circumnavigating the globe to return to its starting point, which it would do if it were following a Great Circle route, but will advance in a spiral course in the northern hemisphere, ending at the North Pole. This can be readily understood if it is appreciated that all meridians converge at the North Pole like the spokes of a wheel and that the flight-path of the plane will make a constant angle of 045° with every meridian it crosses. In question 6 the immediate answer is the North Pole, but it is often overlooked that there are also an infinite number of places near the South Pole where the conditions could be fulfilled. If the reader can imagine a small circle of latitude, 2 km in circumference, close to the South Pole, around which the traveller will move in an easterly direction on the middle leg of his journey, then he has a wide range of starting points which are 2 km north of this circle. Nor is this all, for if the reader can now visualise an even smaller circle of latitude, 1 km in circumference, around which the traveller moves *twice* in order to go due east for 2 km, then another crop of possible starting points, each of them 2 km north of this smaller circle, immediately become available. The total of possible starting points becomes too numerous to estimate.

A third category of maps which enter into school geography are the sketch-maps, so called because they are drawn freehand, unlike the examples of the work of professional cartographers published by the Ordnance Survey or in atlases. This type of map, which appears in textbooks or is drawn on the blackboard or overhead projector, commonly forms the nucleus of a lesson on regional geography. For many years the rubric of the geography paper set for Certificate examinations has exhorted candidates to draw sketch-maps to illustrate their answers wherever possible; this has tended to sustain the importance of the freehand map in formal geography, although it has to be conceded that in the severely limited conditions of an examination the sketch-map becomes little more than a vehicle for transferring information from the candidate to the examiner, and usually it is a map which has been previously memorised by the candidate along with the other factual detail to be duly reproduced in the examination. There is no great attraction in having to copy an existing map from the blackboard or textbook, except to the child who enjoys a mechanical task with opportunities to embellish the finished article using coloured pencils. There is normally more interest aroused and intelligence displayed in compiling a sketch-map from supplied data, whether in prose or statistical form, and examiners are now introducing this style of question into their papers, so that in future sketch-maps are less likely to be mere feats of memory. The outline for the map can be supplied ready-made from a Mapograph roll or Banda machine, or it can be traced from a map in the atlas or textbook, although tracing an outline map into an exercise book is a tedious, time-consuming task. In recent years plastic templates of maps of Britain and other countries and the continents have appeared in stationers' shops, which yield an outline map with reasonable speed. However, none of these devices will provide the pupil with a ready-made copy of the map which has been sketched by the teacher on blackboard or overhead projector, and this will have to be drawn the hard way, freehand. Practice is needed to produce a well-proportioned map outline in reasonable time, but whereas teachers obtain daily practice at the blackboard and soon become proficient at the art, children below the sixth form rarely have more than two or three occasions per week to exercise their skill with a pencil in this direction. I am sympathetic towards the child who experiences some difficulty in copying a map freehand, for not everyone is able to get the correct proportions of a drawing or a map; I can recall that my early attempts in art lessons to draw a standing horse produced a quadruped which resembled a camel falling over backwards. The freehand copying of a map is greatly assisted if a few guidelines are inserted in the initial stages so that the map can be copied piecemeal. In their simplest form these could be a pair of lines intersecting at right angles to form a cross, thereby subdividing the map into four smaller squares or rectangles so that the contents of each quarter can be copied in turn by the pupil. If the area happens to be located within the Tropics a pattern of squares formed by the intersection of lines of latitude and longitude could be used as guidelines, and these need not be erased when the map is completed. Thus a map of West Africa fits neatly into a rectangle formed by the Equator and latitude 20° north, with meridians 20° east and west as the other margins; this can be subdivided into eight squares by inserting three meridians and one parallel at 10° intervals. As the area is reasonably near to the Equator the length of 10° of longitude can be regarded as constant and equal to the distance measured by 10° of latitude. Within this pattern of squares the coastline, main rivers, political boundaries, position of towns and other details of West Africa can be inserted (Figure 9). The scale of the sketch-map can be inferred from the size of each square which has a side length equivalent to ten degrees of latitude and hence represents about 1,100 km. A similar pattern of guidelines can be used for other areas in equatorial latitudes such as the West Indies, East Africa or Indonesia.

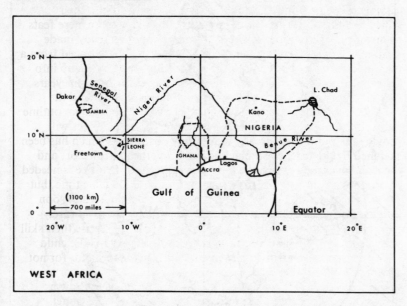

Figure 9 *Guidelines for a sketch-map of West Africa*

Sometimes a circle divided into four sectors by north—south and east—west lines intersecting at the centre will form a useful framework for a sketch-map. For a map of the West Midlands of England centred upon Birmingham, a circle with a radius representing 80 km will have Crewe, Nottingham, Northampton, Gloucester and Hereford on its circumference, while the rivers Severn, Trent and Avon can easily be sketched in place in each quadrant (Figure 10). The geometrical shape of the framework for any map can be varied to suit the region under consideration; South America and the Indian subcontinent, for instance, can be fitted into a pattern of triangles. A few minutes with a school atlas, ruler, pencil and dividers will enable anyone to devise suitable guidelines to assist children in drawing simple sketch-maps of the countries and regions which are studied in school. Some pupils will enjoy devising their own pattern of guidelines as the preliminary to drawing a freehand map. Simplicity in construction is the keynote and if a few important places happen to lie on some of the guidelines, so much the better! Moreover, the exercise will direct their attention towards

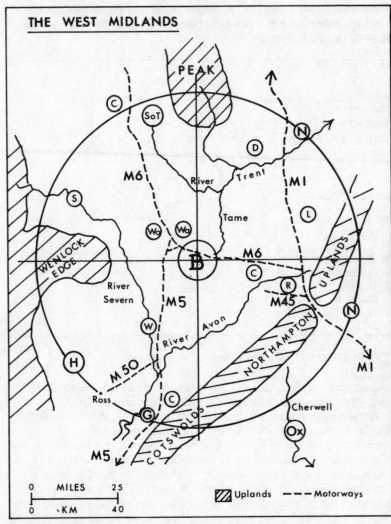

THE WEST MIDLANDS

Figure 10 *Guidelines for a sketch-map of the West Midlands*

some dimensions of the region to be mapped which had not previously been appreciated. For example, France is about 960 km in length from north to south, measured from the Belgian frontier near Dunkirk to the Mediterranean border with Spain south of Perpignan. It is roughly the same in width from west to east, measured from the tip of the Brittany peninsula near Brest to the corner of Alsace north-east of Strasbourg. Paris is situated close to the intersection of these two guidelines and if their extremities are connected, using Bayonne and Monte Carlo as the positions for additional 'corners', a roughly symmetrical six-sided figure provides the framework for a sketch-map of France. Of course, it is understood that some areas are too complex to be drawn easily by amateurs and for these areas duplicated outlines using a Banda machine or a Mapograph roll are the obvious answer. Europe is probably the continent with the most irregular shape for a sketch-map and I confess I find that Britain has the most difficult outline of any country to copy easily – there are too many capes and bays!

REFERENCES

W. G. V. Balchin, 'The representation of true to scale linear values on map projections', *Geography*,|vol. 36, 1951, pp. 120–4.

E. C. Bentley, *Biography for Beginners* (London, Werner Laurie, 1905).

B. Coates (ed.), *Census Atlas of South Yorkshire*, (University of Sheffield, Department of Geography, 1974).

J. P. Cole and N. J. Beynon, *New Ways in Geography*, Book 2, (London, Blackwell, 1973).

J. Disley, *Your Way with Map and Compass* (London, Blond Educational, 1971).

H. J. Mackinder, 'Geography, an art and a philosophy', *Geography*, vol. 27, 1942, p. 123.

W. Pick, 'The school itself as a geographical resource: some ideas', *Teaching Geography*, vol. 5, 1979, pp. 25–7.

Eve Pownall, *The Australia Book*, (London, Methuen, 1953) p. 31.

Rev. R. Turner, *A New and Easy Introduction to Universal Geography* (1779) (London, Salisbury, 10th edn, 1802).

Chapter 3

Excursions into Paronomasia

Although this title might appear to hint at travels in Tartary or some other empty quarter of the Asiatic continent, the explorations to be described here are verbal rather than terrestrial; they relate to a certain dexterity in the use of the mother-tongue which is at once a source of amusement and edification to teachers as well as to their pupils.

A popular form of word-play which emerged at the beginning of the present century is the crossword puzzle. The first one was published in America in 1913 although its compiler was a native-born Englishman from Liverpool. Crosswords began to appear in English newspapers during the 1920s when it was widely thought that they would prove to be a passing craze as ephemeral as the Charleston – another contemporary import from the USA – but they have endured to become a feature of the British way of life, providing entertainment and stimulating thought among people of all ages. On this side of the Atlantic many crosswords are now of a highly sophisticated kind, employing anagrams, puns and ingenious transpositions, so that only the aficionado identifies 'shrewd early invader of Norfolk' (two words, each of five letters) as acute Angle, appreciates that a *carthorse* can upset an *orchestra* or that a *schoolmaster* can turn into *the classroom* and recognises that Mary is capable of extending the oyster season for an additional month (by putting an 'r' in May). Familiarity with geographical names can be an asset when tackling a cryptic crossword puzzle, although in solving the clue 'vegetarian meal about five with a choice in Central America' (eight letters) it is an understanding of the logodaedaly exercised by the compiler which enables the enthusiast to eliminate Honduras and arrive at Salvador as the correct answer. In its simple form, however, the crossword is a test of general knowledge and skill in the use of English and as such it can be used in school as an educational game or as a device for revising work already done. Many geography textbooks written for the less academic pupil now contain crossword puzzles among the varied exercises and 'things to do' which are designed to recall the subject-matter of recent lessons. More gifted pupils can often be persuaded to construct puzzles for their class-mates to solve, with clues and answers based on geographical expressions and place-names, while advocates of integrated studies might encourage their brighter pupils to devise clues requiring knowledge of more than one subject, as in the following example: 'space in Germany becomes a remote Soviet river' (four letters).

Long before the crossword puzzle was invented, however, children were accustomed to playing with words. In their early years, as soon as they begin to acquire rudimentary speech, they regard words as toys and the sounds of the spoken language have a particular appeal. They soon learn to distinguish different meanings of the same word, such as the bark of a dog and the bark of a tree, and tongue-twisters are amusing because of the repetition of letters or sounds, whether they make sense or not, as in 'a noisy noise annoys an oyster'. During their schooldays the uninhibited verbal exchanges of the playground, street or classroom include spoonerisms, tongue-twisters, nonsense rhymes (some of which are used in skipping or bouncing a ball), punning repartee and catch-phrases of great antiquity.

C. W. Kimmins studied several thousand essays written by children of all ages on the subject of amusing sights and stories in order to discover the springs of laughter in young persons. He found that riddles were a popular form of paronomasia among children in primary schools up to the age of 11; during the onset of puberty a falling-off in the appreciation of verbal humour was noticed in boys and girls but this was regained about the age of 15 when the riddle was discarded in favour of more sophisticated puns, including plays on geographical names. One example of the latter, quoted by Kimmins, has since been adapted to form a popular song which has become part of the repertoire of an American television entertainer. In it the names of several states of the Union are thinly disguised in a series of questions and answers, after this fashion:

What did Della wear? – She wore a brand new jersey.
Where has Orry gone? – Ah'll ask her – She's gone to pay her taxes.

The asides of professional comedians are often converted by children into riddles so that they can enjoy them more fully. Thus: 'It won't be long now, as the monkey said when he caught his tail in the bacon-slicer' becomes 'What did the monkey say when he caught his tail in the bacon-slicer?'.

Sometimes the pun forms the basis of juvenile repartee:

'I feel like a long cool drink
That's funny, you don't look like one.'

Occasionally a jingle may have a geographical basis:

'Long legged Italy
Kicked poor Sicily
Right into the middle of the Mediterranean Sea.
Austria and Hungary
Took a bit of Turkey
Dipped it in Greece
Fried it in Japan
And ate it off China.'

Some children in parts of Scotland and northern England manage to bounce a ball rhythmically to the recital of these words.

The impressive feature of these jingles, riddles and repartee is their persistence, for they are absorbed by each generation of children and retailed with relish as if they had been newly invented each time they are uttered. Moreover, they can be remembered long after the child has grown into adulthood, for they are acquired at an impressionable age. Iona and Peter Opie have collected hundreds of these sayings of children in a fascinating book which also contains several maps to show the regional distribution of selected words such as those used by children as a term of truce during play.

Children's comics and Christmas annuals provide a written medium for relating and preserving the word-play of youngsters. Some of these items contain snippets of geographical information which may be retained by the child after more important details, imparted during formal lessons, have been forgotten. A few examples of these include the following:

Teacher: What is the capital of Alaska?
Boy: Please, Miss, Juneau?
Teacher: Of course I do, you cheeky boy.

What do people in British Columbia do with the salmon they catch?
They eat what they can, and they can what they can't.

Can you name the moors of the south-west of England?
Yes, they start with the letters A, B, C, D, E.
What are they?
Austell, Bodmin, Dartmoor, Exmoor.
What about the C?
Oh, that's all around them.

The following joke was popular during the interwar years when

American films about 'gangsters' and prohibition were prominent in British cinemas:

Teacher: What is manufactured in Boston, Massachusetts?
Boy: Boots and shoes.
Teacher: Correct. And what do we get from Chicago?
Boy: Shoots and booze.

From time to time comics include riddles containing a pun on a place-name; here are a few examples:

If a convict escaped from prison, where would he go?
He would go to Hyde in Cheshire.

If a man bought a new television set where would he go?
He would go to Watchet in Somerset.

If you gave your father a present of a new pair of trousers, where would he go?
He would go to Wareham in Dorset.

(An end-of-term competition for the best collection of this type of word-play stimulated an earnest study of the atlas maps of the British Isles among a class of boys who were not particularly keen on the more formal aspects of geography.)
    Another piece of geographical word-play runs something like this:

What did the River Nile say when it saw the concrete-mixers gathering at Aswan?
Well, I'll be dammed!

    Authors and proof-readers can also fall for the charm of this particular pun, for a book concerned with the teaching of geography which was published a few years ago contained a model lesson on glaciation, and on two different pages there was a clearly printed reference to the moraine damned [*sic*] lakes of Snowdonia. However, this error was corrected when the second edition of the book appeared, a few years later.
    It can be argued that the geographical content of this juvenile word-play is trivial and quite unimportant in comparison with the material of formal lessons. Moreover, the mere fact of the persistence of these sayings renders them liable to a charge of being antiquated, especially if they refer to details of human and economic geography. Nevertheless, teachers ought to be aware of this lore of

the classroom and playground; gross inaccuracies of fact can be corrected, and occasionally an item may rise to the surface of the lesson to create an atoll of comic relief in the middle of an ocean of serious dialogue.

In *1066 and All That* Sellar and Yeatman satirised the conventional school history book with its traditional anecdotes about famous people and its potted assessments of reigns and Acts of Parliament as good or bad things. The success of this unorthodox history of the English people appears to have overshadowed a companion volume, *And Now All This*, which Sellar and Yeatman published two years later. In this second book the authors applied their earlier treatment of history to an assortment of subjects including polar exploration, knitting, photography – and geography. The last of these was accorded two chapters in the book, the first being concerned with general principles and global themes while the second was devoted to regional studies of selected 'conceivable' countries. Many children would probably agree with Sellar and Yeatman that there is an excess of geographical things, and accordingly might support the proposal for a 'Perpetual Geographical Holiday' whereby a selected portion of the world map would be declared a zone of 'No Geography' or total 'Geo-Nography'. In this zone all headlands would be decapitated, capes unbuttoned, rivers damned and watersheds dismantled.

Although some of the regional references to famous people and political events have a pre-war flavour which might puzzle younger readers today, these two chapters on geography by Sellar and Yeatman exploit a form of word-play which always appeals to children, whether the reference is to people such as French officials in their sky-blue uniforms or overcôtes d'azur, or to places such as the Alpine zone famous for its climbing and skiing which is known for shorts as the Bareknese Oberland. Moreover, in gently poking fun at the jargon employed by some geographers who write school textbooks, these chapters offer an effective antidote to the pomposity and excessive earnestness which often characterise books written for children.

One form of word-play which is exclusive to the school and examination hall is the 'howler', which is described in the dictionary, somewhat inadequately, as a 'glaring and amusing blunder'. Many of the errors committed by pupils and students are glaring but not amusing – spelling mistakes, for instance, which recur in every generation like an insidious infection: the Rhur coalfield, Niagra Falls, and Ordinance Survey are typical. Then there are errors of identity, whereby the Tropics of Cancer and of Capricorn are confused, or latitude is quoted when it should have been longitude;

these are ordinary, glaring errors which are irritating rather than humorous. In contrast to these the howler possesses certain distinctive qualities:

(1) It is spontaneous and unpremeditated. The class humorist, who offers a facetious comment or definition with the deliberate intention of creating laughter in the lesson, does not perpetrate a howler, for the latter is always made in good faith, usually with seriousness, and often with confidence.

(2) Whether spoken or written, the howler usually contains some incongruity which is not at the time apparent to the person presenting it, but which is at once perceived by the person to whom it is addressed. The humour of the howler lies in the alternative interpretation which can be placed upon the spoken or written words, creating another image for the recipient.

(3) The howler is essentially a product of the learning situation, because it implies that the person committing the blunder is in a subordinate position to the person receiving it. The superior intellectual equipment of the teacher which enables him to perceive the dual interpretation of the answer is contrasted with the limited knowledge of the pupil or student who fails to appreciate the incongruity of his response. A comparable gaffe made by one adult in the company of other adults, whether during work or leisure, would not technically qualify to be called a howler.

(4) Precisely because the howler is produced in the classroom or examination hall, the special environment favours its creation, for it is commonly made by a person under some nervous strain who is aware that he is being placed on trial. The child who is told to stand up in class and give an answer to a question put by the teacher may be unsure of the correct response and therefore apprehensive of the reception which will be accorded his answer by the teacher and by the rest of the class. In a written examination the nervous condition of the candidates is often exacerbated by the time factor, so that even a good candidate may perpetrate written howlers because he knows much more than can be comfortably expressed on paper within the time allowed for completion.

Hitherto the howler has been regarded invariably as a form of entertainment, good for a laugh and little else. Most books of jokes contain a selection of schoolboy howlers and for a number of years several issues of the *Geographical Magazine* have printed examples, without comment, under the significant heading 'Ge-okes'. The howler is rarely regarded as the symptom of a breakdown in communication between teacher and learner, and even more rarely is it conceded that the teacher might be responsible for the error of omission or ambiguity which gave rise to the blunder. A howler is commonly the expression of some fact or concept which was imperfectly learned at the time it was taught, so that when the teacher subsequently seeks to recall that item in a question which he puts to the learner, the phrasing of the response, whether spoken or written, exposes the imperfection of the earlier exchanges between teacher and pupil. Yet if it is the accepted procedure for a teacher to correct non-humorous errors, such as spelling mistakes, made by a pupil, should it not also be desirable for him to investigate the origins of an error which is condoned because it raises a smile? Half a century ago John Adams in a book concerned with errors in school suggested that a howler which cannot be analysed and explained by the teacher indicates an unexplored tract of the pupil's mind, and it is the essence of his craft that the teacher should reduce these tracts to a minimum. Accordingly there would seem to be some justification for analysis and classification of the various types of geographical howler, with comments on their causes and prevention. The examples which follow have been gathered from various sources including several which have been printed in the *Geographical Magazine* as 'Ge-okes' and others from the collection made by a retired university teacher who conceals his true identity behind a pseudonym. Could it be that 'Ben Trovato' conveys a hint as to the authenticity of his howlers? There is a Spanish proverb which runs 'se non è vero, è ben trovato' – 'if they are not true they have been well invented'. These I acknowledge with gratitude. Most of the remainder have been accumulated by me over many years of teaching and examining and are published here for the first time.

TAXONOMY OF GEOGRAPHICAL HOWLERS

The characteristics of each type of howler, with appropriate examples, are followed by comments on the situations which predispose the learner to commit these errors, together with suggested procedures for preventing their recurrence.

Type 1
A misspelling of the correct word produces another word with a very different meaning from the one intended.

Examples:
(*a*) Along the banks of the Fraser River in British Columbia there are huge canaries.

(*b*) If you climb to the top of Vesuvius you can see the creator smoking.

(*c*) Glaziers work very slowly but the destruction they do is enormous.

(*d*) The interior of Ireland is a bogey country.

(*e*) Cattle ranchers in the prairies were superseeded by the arable farmer.

(*f*) When a volcano erupts it throws up malt and larva.

Whenever he gets on to his favourite topic of arid landscapes he always has a pediment in his speech

Comment: This type of error is essentially a slip of the pen and is only revealed in the writing of it. Accordingly it occurs in examination scripts, homework and in notes dictated in class. The howler may originate through carelessness in writing, but more often it is due to the writer being unfamiliar with the word in question. Whenever a teacher introduces a class to a technical term or phrase for the first time, it should be written boldly on the chalkboard or overhead projector, pronounced aloud, spelled out and explained clearly before the lesson proceeds, so that pupils are familiar with the word when it has to be written down. Many of these errors are caused as much by the negligence of the teacher as by the carelessness of the pupil.

Type 2
The wrong word is used in place of the correct one, which it resembles phonetically.

Examples:
(*a*)   The British Isles have a temporary climate.
(*b*)   In Russia there are vast carnivorous forests.
(*c*)   Harsh living conditions account for the negligent population of Labrador.
(*d*)   The dry wind blowing from the Sahara is called the Manhattan.
(*e*)   Calcutta has a laxative climate which makes the inhabitants unable to work for long.
(*f*)   When a good Buddhist dies he hopes to reach the state of Nevada.

Comment: This error can be written or spoken. It commonly occurs when the class is introduced to a new word or technical term which the teacher does not emphasise sufficiently by spelling it aloud or by writing it on the blackboard. In consequence the pupil mentally confuses the new word with another one better known and which sounds correct. Notes dictated too rapidly to a class frequently produce this type of howler, a characteristic which it shares with Type 1. In some cases it is tempting to conjecture that there is not only a phonetic resemblance between the right and the wrong word used, but also a deep-seated association of ideas; in example (*b*), perhaps the key to the error lies in the word 'taiga' which may have been in the mind of the person committing the blunder?

Type 3
This is a badly phrased statement whereby clumsy or obscure wording yields an alternative interpretation.

Examples:
(*a*)   Nomads are people who never live long anywhere.
(*b*)   The Australians are doing their utmost to make water in the desert regions.
(*c*)   The population of Africa is increasing very rapidly with the help of the Europeans.
(*d*)   An isotherm is a line on a map joining places where the temperature is always the same.
(*e*)   On the coalfields of Britain the people are very dense.
(*f*)   Chicago lies at the bottom of Lake Michigan.

Comment: This error can be committed in speech or writing and generally arises when the performer is nervous. It is often found in examination scripts and can occur in class when a pupil is suddenly called upon to answer a question put by the teacher. The last of the above examples is a consequence of faulty map-reading and occurs when a pupil fails to appreciate the reality which lies behind the symbolism of the map. By the same defect, Dublin is located 'just above the Wicklow Mountains' and Denmark is 'underneath Norway'.

Type 4
Two discrete themes or terms become erroneously associated in a confused statement.

Examples:
(*a*)   The days are longer in summer because the heat makes them expand.
(*b*)   The London Clay was deposited during the Plasticene period.
(*c*)   Explorers went by boat up the river Nile to the cataracts and continued their journey in Sudan chairs.
(*d*)   Stirling is famous for its fine silver.
(*e*)   Relief rain is the rain that falls at the end of a long dry period.
(*f*)   Sheep are shorn on the Canterbury Plains and exported in a chilled condition.

Comment: This form of geographical zeugma often emerges in writing during an examination when a harassed candidate, pressed for time and uncertain of his facts, brings together two items of knowledge which appear to him at the time to have something in common. His highly nervous condition leads him into mental word-play; observe, for instance, the interpretation put upon the word 'relief' in example (*e*). The same type of error can be uttered aloud in class when a pupil is suddenly called upon to answer a question for which he is inadequately prepared, and he is startled into making a garbled response.

Type 5
This is an absurd statement resulting from hasty expression, muddled thinking and inadequate knowledge.

Examples:
(*a*)   In the southern hemisphere Christmas Day falls in June.
(*b*)   At first the Great Lakes—St Lawrence waterway only went as far inland as Montreal.
(*c*)   Natal has a heavy summer rainfall but most of it falls in winter.

(*d*)   Few of the Spanish rivers are navigable because they flow away from the sea.
(*e*)   RF 1:126,720 means that in the first month (January) there is a rainfall of 126,720 mm.
(*f*)   In summer the earth is nearer the Equator than in the winter.

Comment: Nonsense statements of this kind can be perpetrated by intelligent pupils when writing under the stress of examination conditions, or by weaker brethren at any time.

Type 6

An invented word is substituted for the correct one.

Examples:
(*a*)   Aircraft provide a link for the scattered Eskimos and traders who live in the frozen Canadian archeapology.
(*b*)   There is little ribbonation along the roads in this area.
(*c*)   The lower-lying land is used arably.
(*d*)   The Cantabrians are prodimently unpopulated.
(*e*)   The dome-shaped masses of granite on Dartmoor are called baccoliths.
(*f*)   Cotton-growing in the southern states has suffered from the depredations of the beevil.

Comment: I can vouch for the authenticity of the first four examples which I encountered in marking Advanced Level GCE scripts. This type of error is more widespread in essays and examination papers than many people imagine and it arises from the attempt to employ exotic words or pseudo-technical expressions in order to make the written answer appear more impressive. However, one ought to be charitable; before we condemn 'ribbonation' as a substitute for 'ribbon development' in example (*b*) above, should we not admit that it is no more offensive than terms such as 'sedentarisation', 'desertification' or 'villagisation' which have now crept into print in advanced university texts and geographical journals of repute? It may well be that the schoolboy howlers of today become the accepted 'ge-argon' of tomorrow.

'Baccolith' in the above group is presumably a hybrid developed from bathylith and laccolite; mongrels of this kind may irritate rather than amuse the recipient, who might consider it to be on a base level with flagrant spelling errors such as Niagra or Rhur. Some of the examples of Type 6 seem to hover on the delicate divide separating errors which amuse from those which annoy, and it could be argued that not all of these coined expressions are fully developed howlers. Perhaps, recalling the etymology of 'peneplain', they could justifiably be termed 'penehowlers'?

In his study of the topics and incidents which provoke laughter in young persons, Kimmins noted that children become more critical in their observations after the age of 11. At the secondary school stage they are amused by comical incidents which expose the stupidity of some of their class-mates and by the verbal exchanges between teacher and individual pupils, particularly when those in authority give instructions which are badly phrased. Two examples will illustrate typical situations. A boy was discovered eating sweets and at the same time was slumped in his desk so that his legs projected forward to annoy the occupant of the desk in front of him. In reproving him the teacher said 'Take those sweets out of your mouth and put your feet in'. This caused much laughter in class, as did the response of the girl who was asked during a lesson on religious knowledge to quote a Commandment containing four words, and replied 'Keep off the grass'. In short, teachers as well as children can make howlers, and adolescents are just as capable as adults of seeing the funny side of a blunder made by one of their class-mates. Since the ability to appreciate sophisticated word-play depends upon one's knowledge and intellectual development, then the exegesis of a howler in class would advance the education of those weaker pupils who, upon first hearing it, were not amused.

REFERENCES

J. Adams, *Errors in School* (London, University of London Press, 1927).

C. W. Kimmins, *The Springs of Laughter* (London, Methuen, 1928).

I. and P. Opie, *The Lore and Language of Schoolchildren* (London, Oxford University Press, 1959).

W. C. Sellar and R. J. Yeatman, *1066 and All That* (London, Methuen, 1930).

W. C. Sellar and R. J. Yeatman, *And Now All This* (London, Methuen, 1932).

Ben Trovato, *Best Howlers* (London, Wolfe, 1970).

Chapter 4

Image and Reality

During the years they attend school children acquire facts and attitudes about the countries and peoples of the world, including their own homeland, from two sources. One of these is the programme of formal geography lessons which can present the subject-matter in a logical, comprehensive and even stimulating manner – depending on the abilities of the teachers who are conducting the course, and the range of equipment and time at their disposal. Coexistent with this formal presentation of geography is another reservoir of information and impression which contributes to the child's understanding of his environment and neighbours, a source of fact and figment which may be haphazard, fragmentary and often lacking in impartiality, yet which may make a stronger impact on the child's senses and memory precisely because it is acquired informally and indeed is often deliberately sought. In this second category are included the conversations of parents and adults (not necessarily directed at the child, for the overheard exchanges between adults are often the ones which the child recalls most vividly), advertisements of all kinds, daily and weekly papers and magazines, children's comics and other works of fiction or fact such as school stories or encyclopaedias; the radio, television and cinema programmes, letters and postcards from friends and relatives, and experiences of travel, during holidays, or when parents move home to another part of the country. The personal observations and impressions of travellers, whether sustained or casual, yield images which differ both in quality and impact from those acquired at second-hand by way of books, pictures or conversation. It does not matter how accurate and detailed may be the impression you have formed of San Francisco or Sunderland as a result of information you have acquired from others; your image of the city will be dramatically different after you have personally visited it and experienced it for yourself.

Teachers of geography can in large measure control the presentation of facts and attitudes during lessons in school, but they cannot hope to regulate the extent or reliability of the impressions which are absorbed by their pupils informally at other times. They can, however, gauge the proportion of the intake from these two sources by conducting periodical tests with a view to correcting any prejudices or faulty information which the children may have acquired. When a class is about to begin the formal study of a new region or country, be it East Anglia or West Germany, it is often a useful opening gambit for the teacher to invite pupils to say what ideas or phrases spring immediately to their minds when the name of that area is mentioned. If a similar exercise is conducted a few weeks after the study of the area has been completed, a comparison of the two lists of topics will reveal how far the teacher's formal lessons have modified the pupils' ideas about that area. John Haddon carried out tests of this kind with his geography classes at an independent boarding school. He reported that to the boys and girls in his class France consisted of the Eiffel Tower, the Folies Bergères (which no one could spell correctly), Christian Dior and the Riviera; its inhabitants were a race of fickle, excitable, politically obsessed people who dined and wined magnificently, wearing berets, in the midst of unmentionable plumbing ... In the southern hemisphere, by contrast, the South Africans broke off from fighting the Boer War to eat oranges, make fortunes from gold and diamonds and oppress the 'natives' under a government as merciless as the ever-present sun. Unfortunately Haddon conducted his inquiries as a single exercise at the conclusion of his lessons on the countries under review, so that he was not able to assess the influence of his teaching upon the attitudes and prejudices which his pupils had previously acquired from other sources.

It would be quite unfair to assume that the faulty images concerning places and people which are held by children have been derived mainly from parents who are lacking in schooling and intelligence, for mistaken beliefs of this kind are also found among educated professional people. The Sheffield evening paper, *The Star*, carried a report on 16 May 1975 that about a hundred members of staff employed by one of the leading banks in London had met together to reject emphatically a proposal that they should move to work for the same bank in Sheffield. A union official said privately that often it was simply prejudice against Sheffield. He continued: 'They have an image of smoke-stacks and dark satanic mills that is very difficult to dispel. We have pointed out, in fairness, that Sheffield is not like that, but they won't be convinced, and it is our duty to follow their wishes.' The sequel to this news item is that about a year afterwards these London bank employees were persuaded, if not convinced, that Sheffield has a bright side, and they consented to the transfer. Poor Sheffield! It has for a long time had a bad image among those Englishmen who live south of the Trent. In 1830 William Cobbett rode on horseback from Leeds to

Sheffield and was moved to describe the 'horrible splendour' of the furnaces in the South Yorkshire coalfield. 'They call it Black Sheffield, and black enough it is', he wrote in his journal. Almost exactly a hundred years after Cobbett made his rural rides another observer of the contrasts between the north and the south of Britain spent a winter's afternoon in the lunar landscape of slagheaps which formed the dreadful environs of Wigan during the Depression of the 1930s. After painting a grim picture of the dereliction on the Lancashire coalfield – 'a world from which vegetation had been banished; nothing existed except smoke, shale, ice, mud, ashes and foul water', George Orwell continued: 'but even Wigan is beautiful compared with Sheffield. Sheffield, I suppose, could justly claim to be called the ugliest town in the Old World ...'.

Thirty years after Orwell had made his urban ride along the road to Wigan Pier another writer, Geoffrey Moorhouse, rejected the traditional boundary of the Trent as the divide between north and south in Britain; he suggested that one England lies within an hour's journey by fast train from central London, and the other England is the whole of the country located outside that circle. He had harsh words for the fall-out of industrial soot at Rawmarsh near Rotherham in 1961, but confessed that Sheffield had amenities which were not appreciated by people living in the south of England: bold developments in municipal architecture, with grouse moors, lakes well patronised by sailing clubs, and ski-slopes close to the western edge of the city. In the years which have elapsed since Moorhouse wrote his book Sheffield has made strenuous efforts to improve its image and during the summer of 1979 'Welcome Home' celebrations were held which attracted more than a thousand expatriates from twenty-nine different countries. Many of these former residents commented favourably on the transformation which had been effected in the appearance of the city in recent years and the warmth of the welcome accorded them by the present-day inhabitants of Sheffield.

Prejudiced views of the north of England which are held by many people living in the London area were humorously conveyed in map-form by a teacher in a Doncaster school who originally came from Wimbledon. The map was distributed by Doncaster and District Development Council in a light-hearted attempt to attract more industry to Yorkshire (Figure 11). I first saw this map when it was reproduced in the *Sunday Times* on 30 January 1972; since that date it has appeared in *Mental Maps* by Gould and White and in at least one textbook for use in schools. The book by Gould and White examines the geography of perception and studies the images (as distinct from the objective facts) which people acquire of other countries, or other parts of their own country.

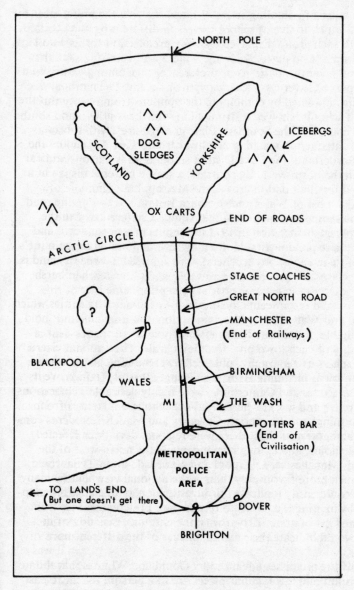

Figure 11: *How Londoners visualise the north of Britain*

It contains a fascinating series of maps showing the preferences for places in which to live of school-leavers in different parts of Britain. Although each group displayed a strong predilection for its own local region – there's no place like home – there was a striking similarity between the various patterns of preference, even among youngsters as far apart as Inverness, Aberystwyth and Kent. The national viewpoint, obtained by combining the opinions from twenty-three different schools, showed a strong liking for the southern and south-western counties, 'the Southern Plateau of Desire', with subsidiary spurs of satisfaction reaching northwards into East Anglia and the Welsh Borderland; the Lake District stood as an isolated island of choice in the north-west. By contrast, a strong national dislike was displayed for the London area – 'the Metropolitan Sinkhole', the Midlands, most of Wales and northern Britain.

At an evening session during the Annual Conference of the Geographical Association in 1972 the results of a postal questionnaire previously submitted by several hundred members (most of them geography teachers) were analysed in order to discuss the concept of the group image and to suggest how teachers might conduct exercises in class on spatial perception. One part of this inquiry invited respondents to study a list of about fifty towns in England and Wales and on the assumption that a satisfactory job was available, to indicate their personal opinion of the residential desirability of each town on a five-point scale. The national view of these teachers of geography, obtained by combining all the replies, was that towns including Bath, Cambridge, Bristol, Oxford, York, Norwich, Exeter and Canterbury, were highly desirable as places in which to live and work, whereas Salford, Stoke-on-Trent, Bradford, Hull, Birmingham, Liverpool, Coventry and Manchester were highly undesirable. Nevertheless, there were regional deviations from the national choice, and among respondents in the north-west of England, Manchester, Liverpool and Newcastle-upon-Tyne were rated much more favourably than in the national viewpoint. A teacher could easily replicate this investigation among a class in school by inviting the pupils to record their preferences on a duplicated list of about fifty towns; the ensuing discussion of the results would indicate their mental images of the different parts of Britain.

One of the premisses advanced by Gould and White is that the more distant and less familiar places are to a person, the more distorted and inaccurate are likely to be his impressions of those places. It is important to realise how powerful these impressions can become, for once individuals or groups of people develop an image of a place, they are convinced of its reality and imagination influences their actions. For example, during the first half of the nineteenth century most Americans believed that the plains between the meridian of longitude 100° west and the crest of the Rocky Mountains were a desert. Numerous histories, atlases, geographies and journals of explorers published between 1820 and 1850 boldly printed 'GREAT AMERICAN DESERT' across the map of the western United States, east of the Rockies, and it became a reality in the minds of the people at the time. So real was this belief that Jefferson Davis, who was United States Secretary of War from 1855 to 1857, obtained an appropriation of 30,000 dollars from Congress in 1855 to import two ship-loads of camels from Turkey. These camels were used by the army for transport in western Texas for a number of years, but their eventual disappearance is perhaps a silent commentary on the inadequacy of the terrain; the Great American Desert was a mirage which existed only in the minds of the men from the East. Far more effective than camels in the conquest of the Great Plains were barbed wire, windmills and six-shooters, a story that is dramatically told by Walter Prescott Webb in his classic history of the American West.

Images exist about people as well as about places and these too can be transmitted from adults to children both directly in conversation and teaching and indirectly through the media. Novels which have become classics can exert a powerful influence upon readers and it has been said that many Russians derive their impressions of modern England from translations of the novels of Charles Dickens. However, it is not only upon continental readers that the influence of English fiction is most potent, for we in England absorb the mental images created by our own novelists. D. C. D. Pocock has shown how fiction writers over the last hundred years or so, from Charlotte Bronte and Mrs Gaskell to John Osborne and John Braine, have emphasised the industrial squalor, the ugly townscapes, the rawness of the climate and the hard unsentimental nature of the inhabitants of northern England to present a picture which in many respects is now inaccurate. The impressions conveyed by these fictional writings are rendered even more effective when they become adapted for the television screen and, as Pocock observes in his article, success in this medium can actually create a demand for the book of the series where none previously existed!

Stage plays and cinema films may also perpetuate impressions of the customs among other nationalities which have become old-fashioned or obsolete. A vivid illustration of this was conveyed to me during travels in America some years ago. I was accompanied by my wife and children and we had camped overnight in a state park on the banks of the Platte River in Nebraska. The next morning we entered a restaurant in the nearby town of Grand Island to have breakfast. A young college student who was working as a waitress during the summer vacation took our order and realised from our speech that we were British. When she returned with the food she asked my wife, 'Do you miss your kidneys?'. Somewhat puzzled by this question, we asked her to explain more fully, and it emerged that she firmly believed that ordinary English people still consumed kidneys for breakfast in the manner of the upper classes so charmingly portrayed in the plays of Oscar Wilde around the turn of the century. Having been corrected on one item our young waitress then inquired almost apprehensively, 'And do you not eat muffins at tea-time?'. This question recalled for us a visit to the cinema which we had made in Ann Arbor, Michigan, only a few weeks previously, when we saw a British film entitled *Murder She Said*. The story was based on one of the novels of Agatha Christie, in which Dame Margaret Rutherford played the part of the amateur detective, Miss Marple, and surely enough, although the setting was modern, Miss Marple and her friend had muffins for tea! Film producers often portray caricatures of national types which convey an untrue picture to audiences in other countries.

It is not only moving pictures projected on to the screen which can convey impressions of people and places; the same is true of still pictures, whether they appear as illustrations in books and magazines, as advertisements upon billboards or as paintings in art galleries. There have been investigations into the reaction of children to *geographical* pictures, for example the research conducted some years ago by M. Long, but hitherto little attention has been paid to the influence upon children of well-known paintings. There is possibly scope for some exploration of this medium, seeing that most schools now have prints of the work of famous artists hanging in the corridors and halls of the building. To what extent do children living in the south of England derive their impressions of the north from the townscapes of chimneys and canals with spindly people parading in the cobbled streets of Salford, made popular by L. S. Lowry? How far do children in northern counties create an image of the appearance of rural Essex from the paintings made by Constable of Flatford Mill and Dedham Lock in the Stour Valley at the beginning of the nineteenth century? To youngsters who have not visited these counties the artist's impressions may be accepted as reality.

The authors of children's books often portray stereotypes of people in other lands and adopt a patronising tone towards people of a different colour. David Milner has commented on the attitudes towards negroes and Chinese which are displayed in books by Arthur Ransome, in the adventures of Golliwogg by B. and F. Upton, the

stories about Little Black Sambo by H. Bannerman, the Doctor
Dolittle books by H. Lofting, or in the adventures of the
indefatigable Biggles related by Captain W. E. Johns. Some years
ago George Orwell wrote an article on boys' weeklies in which he
pointed out that invariably foreigners were portrayed in them as
stereotypes: the Frenchman is excitable, wears a pointed beard and
gesticulates wildly, Spaniards and Mexicans are sinister and
treacherous, Chinese wear pigtails, are inscrutable, and shuffle
silently along, whereas Swedes and Danes are big, kind-hearted, but
often stupid. Orwell claimed that the outlook of many of the
schoolboy stories of the 1930s was that of the comfortable middle-
class world of the pre-1914 era, with working-class Englishmen and
all foreigners portrayed as either comic or sinister characters; the
setting for an adventure story, as distinct from a school story, was
invariably some remote part of the world – Alaska, Australia or the
Arctic – but never the homeland or Western Europe. According to
recent researches undertaken by psychologist Nicholas Tucker, the
stereotyping of foreign nationalities and the out-of-date settings for
adventure stories are features which persist in boys' comics even at
the present time. Nevertheless, television programmes may provide a
modern corrective influence to the errors and distortions of boys'
weeklies, for in this medium adventures take place in the home
country as well as in some remote ex-colony, and today English
villains are just as likely to use a knife or karate chop on their victim
as did the Mexicans and Japanese in stories written before the war.
The behaviour of the English hero has also changed. When
thousands of American servicemen were drafted to Britain during the
Second World War they were each given a little booklet of
information and advice about the British and their way of life
prepared by the War Department in Washington, DC. Some of these
observations read a little strangely today! 'You will find that English
crowds at football or cricket matches are more orderly and more
polite to the players than American crowds.' Times have changed,
and not only the English crowds but the players have become more
demonstrative too – instead of being tight-lipped and apparently
unperturbed at events during a game, they gesticulate fiercely and
when a goal is scored or a wicket falls they leap into the air and
embrace their team-mates with a great show of affection.

What can the geography teacher do to correct the faulty images
and exaggerated stereotypes of people in other lands which are
absorbed by children from the popular media and other sources
outside school? Writing about attitudes of children to other
nationalities, John Carnie reported that when 500 geography
teachers, university lecturers and sixth-formers were invited to put in

rank order thirty statements on the value of learning geography in
school, first choice on average was given to the assertion that
'geography deepens the pupils' appreciation of other people's way of
life' whereas the statement that 'the study of geography helps to
foster international goodwill' was ranked nineteenth. It is not clear
whether one infers from this evidence that the more you get to know
other people and their ways of life, the less you like them, but it
would suggest that geography teachers tend to disclaim responsibility
for promoting international goodwill among their pupils. It has not
always been thus. During the wave of idealism and faith in the
League of Nations which followed the First World War the hope was
often expressed that geography in school would encourage a sane
approach to political, social and international problems in the
world – James Fairgrieve's dictum on the function of school
geography which he expressed in his influential book *Geography in
School* in 1926 is relevant in this context: 'The function of school
geography is to train future citizens to imagine accurately the
conditions of the great world stage and so help them to think sanely
about political and social problems in the world around.' Since the
end of the Second World War, however, patriotism appears to have
lost ground among teachers as well as with children, except for the
campaign to conserve national resources. Instead, more attention is
directed towards creating 'citizens of the world' who will be
concerned with conducting a war on want and attending to the needs
of the underdeveloped nations.

The formal geography taught in school is not necessarily free from
bias. Teachers may strive to present an impartial viewpoint of
countries whose recent history and economic development have not
been lacking in controversy, yet in the very selection of topics for
study and discussion in class they may unconsciously lean in one
direction rather than another.

Many find it difficult to be impartial when the topic for study in
class is the social and economic condition of white and black people
in South Africa, the dissensions between Arabs and Israelis in the
Middle East or the treatment by their respective governments of
ethnic minority groups such as the Indians in North America or the
aborigines in Australia. Earlier generations of pupils were taught to
absorb unquestioningly the facts conveyed to them by their teachers
or textbooks but in recent years it has become fashionable to
encourage pupil participation in lively discussion of controversial
topics which were once discreetly glossed over. Thus the Schools'
Council Curriculum Development Project entitled 'Geography for
the Young School Leaver', which was adopted in many secondary
schools after 1970, brought pupils face to face with politically

It's difficult to teach that little dreamer any geography – he lives in a world of his own

contentious topics such as immigration, unemployment and housing in large cities. W. E. Marsden has indicated in an article on 'Stereotyping and Third World Geography' that if the modern trend is to inject geography lessons with problem issues this must be done without attempting to teach pupils values or to develop attitudes among them. But this may be difficult to achieve if the issues arouse interest among the children. Furthermore, the geography textbooks used in school – many of them written by teachers of long experience – may contain some bias or error of fact. Stephen Hatch examined a number of textbooks in history and geography which were being used in London comprehensive schools, and he found several instances where races and nationalities were grossly stereotyped. The same theme formed the subject of newspaper comment in the *Guardian* recently which was taken up by J. A. Binns in an article on the crucial role played by the media in moulding our perceptions of foreign countries and their inhabitants. He offers some suggestions for dispelling the myths and stereotypes about Third World countries which children acquire outside school. Happily there are now several geographical bodies in various countries which are actively seeking to correct the distorted images which appear in school textbooks. The International Society for Educational Information, with headquarters in Tokyo, has compiled several useful bulletins which help a teacher to convey the correct image of Japan. The first of these booklets, issued in 1960, presented extracts culled from textbooks on Japan which were written for use in the primary and secondary schools of thirty-six different countries, and each group of extracts is followed by comments and gentle corrections, some of this enlightenment being in the form of photographs or maps. The commentary is edited by Professor Ishida of the Department of Geography in Hitotsubashi University, Tokyo, who mentions, for example, that very few Japanese under the age of 60 have ever ridden in a rickshaw, (a vehicle which has now disappeared from the streets of Japanese cities); that most Japanese homes are not constructed of wood, paper and bamboo; that fish do not teem in the coastal waters surrounding Japan, moreover the use of cormorants with rings around their throats to catch fish in the inland rivers is merely a tourist attraction limited to a small number of places; finally, that Sapporo, not Hakodate, is the largest city in the island of Hokkaido.

Factual errors are less likely to occur in a textbook which has been written by a native of the country or someone who has made frequent visits to the area. With this point in mind E. C. Marchant edited a book on the countries of Europe in which each chapter was written by a geographer of the country concerned. More recently, an Anglo-Dutch Conference on the Mutual Revision of Geography Textbooks, held at Utrecht in the Netherlands, revealed that both countries are given distorted images of each other. It would appear that British teachers and textbook writers can obtain accurate information about the Netherlands from the Information and Documentation Centre for the Geography of the Netherlands in Utrecht, but that reciprocal facilities are not available to Dutch teachers and authors, for there is no equivalent information centre in Britain. This may explain the 'somewhat outdated view of Britain as an old industrial country of grey industrial towns swathed in smog' which appears in some of the Dutch textbooks.

An image of a place can be conveyed by some form of advertisement or slogan which is usually devised to attract rather than repel the visitor. Thus the keen cool winds experienced in the holiday resorts along the east coast of Britain are given a therapeutic quality when they are described in the phrase 'Skegness is so bracing!'. Americans offer an image of the various states of the

Union in slogans which adorn their car number plates, for in addition to the name of the state in which the car was registered, most plates carry a few descriptive words to advertise some feature of that state. Some are faintly geographical such as:

Arizona   – Grand Canyon State
Florida   – Sunshine State
Georgia   – Peach State
Michigan   – Great Lakes State
             (it used to be Water Wonderland)
Minnesota   – 10,000 Lakes
Nebraska   – The Beef State
Wisconsin   – America's Dairyland

The reference may be historical, as in:

Alabama   – Heart of Dixie
Illinois   – Land of Lincoln

or it may be the invitation to businessmen conveyed by:

Arkansas   – Land of Opportunity

More often however, it is designed to attract the tourist, whether from another state or another country:

Louisiana   – Sportsmen's Paradise
Maine   – Vacationland
New Mexico   – Land of Enchantment

whilst there is something down-to-earth about:

Idaho   – Famous potatoes

Some years ago, when we were camping in the Rocky Mountains and Pacific states, strangers would stroll over and introduce themselves to us after seeing the Michigan plates on our Chevrolet, with the excuse that they had once lived in Michigan or they had relatives who were still living there . . . For our part, the farther west we travelled, the deeper became the affection we felt for any other car on the road or camp-site which also carried Michigan plates. Paul Jennings, in a *Telegraph Sunday Magazine* article, once suggested that it might enliven touring around Britain if we advertised features of each county on car registration plates after the style of the Americans. It would at least do more to illustrate regional contrasts to travellers than the current system of a combination of alphabetical letters which conceal the location of the licensing authority! Here are a few suggestions which he made:

Cornwall   – Celts without kilts
Derbyshire   – Best-dressed wells
Essex   – Where creek meets creek
Lincolnshire   – Potatoes and poachers
Norfolk   – Potatoes and jackets
Surrey   – 10,000 tennis clubs
Sussex   – Stockbrokers' paradise
Yorkshire   – Land of the Pudding

The Welsh counties, noted for intense poetry and patriotism, might adopt more forthright slogans such as:

Caernarvonshire (now Gwynedd)   – Myndd your owain bysnys
Glamorgan   – See Cardiff and Dai

It might prove to be a congenial end-of-term exercise to invite a class of young geographers, given a few of the above examples, to concoct slogans for the remaining counties in Britain. It would serve to draw their attention to some of the outstanding geographical features of each county!

There are signs that regional characteristics of cultural traits in Britain are being strengthened rather than diminished in recent years. Numerous local radio stations have been established which devote considerable programme-time to descriptions of local customs, speech, events and personalities in their respective neighbourhoods, while the regional television stations perform a similar function for a wider area. Some news-readers now reveal a regional accent in place of the neutral 'BBC speech' which was formerly essential to their calling, and the commercial cinema is probably less successful than radio and television in preserving local dialects and customs, while organisations such as the Black Country Society preserve the regional consciousness of specific areas and intensify local pride. Moreover, the extension of secondary and higher education to a much greater proportion of the country's youth since 1944 does not appear to have diminished the preference of school-leavers and university students for their own particular regional dialect in their daily speech.

It is curious that alongside the development of the scientific, quantitative, objective approach to geography which has been a feature of recent years there has been a realisation of the importance of the subjective, personal, impressionistic approach, so that not merely people and places as they are but as we imagine them to be, now merit serious consideration. Studies of the geography of perception have demonstrated that images can have the force of reality in motivating people to act in certain ways; it thus becomes a function of geographical study to examine the degree to which our images do not coincide with reality. A well-known phrase of Robert Burns runs:

> O wad some Pow'r the giftie gi'e us
> To see oursel's as others see us.

It may perhaps be salutary if on occasion we pray for the gift 'to see others as they see themselves'.

REFERENCES

J. A. Binns, 'How "we" see "them" – some thoughts on Third World teaching', *Teaching Geography*, vol. 4, 1979, pp. 176–7.

J. Carnie, 'Children's attitudes to other nationalities', in *New Movements in the Study and Teaching of Geography*, ed. N. Graves (London, Temple Smith, 1972), ch. 10.

W. Cobbett, *Rural Rides* (1830), ed. Pitt Cobbett (London, Reeves & Turner, 1893), Vol. 2.

J. Fairgrieve, *Geography in School* (London, University of London Press, 1926), p. 18.

P. Gould and R. White, *Mental Maps* (Harmondsworth, Penguin, 1974).

J. Haddon, 'A view of foreign lands', *Geography*, vol. 45, 1960, pp. 286–9.

S. Hatch, 'Coloured people in school textbooks', *Race*, vol. 4, 1962, pp. 63–72.

Information and Documentation Centre, *Final Report on the Revision of Geography Textbooks* (IDC for Geography of Netherlands, Utrecht, 1975).

R. Ishida (ed.), *Understanding Japan*, Bulletin No. 1 of the International Society for Educational Information (Tokyo, 1960).

M. Long, 'Research in picture study. The reaction of grammar school pupils to geographical pictures', *Geography*, vol. 46, 1961, pp. 322–37.

E. C. Marchant (ed.), *The Countries of Europe as Seen by Their Geographers* (London, Harrap, 1970).

W. E. Marsden, 'Stereotyping and Third World geography', *Teaching Geography*, vol. 1, 1976, pp. 228–31.

D. Milner, *Children and Race* (Harmondsworth, Penguin, 1975).

G. Moorhouse, *Britain in the Sixties: The Other England*, (Harmondsworth, Penguin, 1964), pp. 154–9.

George Orwell, *The Road to Wigan Pier* (London, Gollancz, 1937), ch. 7; 'Boys' weeklies' (written 1939), in *The Collected Essays, Journalism and*

Letters of George Orwell, ed. S. Orwell and I. Angus, Vol. 1 (London, Secker & Warburg, 1968), pp. 460–84.

D. C. D. Pocock, 'The novelist's image of the north', *Trans. Institute of British Geographers* (new series), vol. 4, 1979, pp. 62–76.

N. Tucker, 'A new look at the British comic', *Where* (Cambridge, ACE, November 1976), pp. 291–3, 326–9.

W. P. Webb, *The Great Plains* (New York, Grosset & Dunlap, 1931).

Chapter 5

Testing, Testing, One, Two, Three...

There is a profound contrast between the pleasure which children
derive from listening to quiz programmes on radio or television and
the distaste which they evince for similar tests of knowledge which
are conducted during lessons in school. Fundamentally this reflects a
difference of purpose. Children enjoy watching or participating in
tests on television because such exercises are conceived and
conducted as entertainment; there are rewards for giving the right
answers but no reprimands for giving the wrong ones. In school, on
the other hand, if a pupil fails to answer a question correctly there is
usually a verbal reproof administered by the teacher and the failure
may even be recorded on a mark sheet, to be used in evidence when
rank order lists of the class are compiled at the end of the term. How
many adults would be willing to attend evening classes during the
week or church services on Sunday if they were subjected to similar
treatment? There is a difference, of course; the adults form an
audience of volunteers who might well withdraw their attendance if
they were made to feel uncomfortably ignorant during a lecture or
sermon, whereas children in school are mostly conscripts who attend
by law, rather than by inclination. Testing in school is a device to
ensure that the majority have reached a reasonable level of
understanding and competence; it enables the teacher to praise the
proficient, jog the indolent and identify weaknesses in his own
teaching. Above all, it provides a periodical assessment of the child's
performance which marks a stage in progress towards the
culmination of the course – the final examination or certification. In
some schools testing is pursued with a zeal akin to fanaticism so that
sufficient tell-tale marks can be accumulated to place the pupils in
rank order and promote or relegate the extremes at the end of each
term, like the annual reshuffle in April of teams in the four divisions
of the Association Football League. But approval for this custom is
not universal; many teachers feel that excessive grading is degrading.

   Testing in school derives much of its importance from the
emphasis placed on certification, for prestige in British education has
been closely related to examinations for more than a hundred years.
Teachers in elementary schools were examined by the state from 1846
onwards, the College of Preceptors organised examinations for boys

and girls a few years later, and the Royal Military Academy instituted selective tests for army entrance in 1855. Shortly afterwards Oxford and Cambridge began to offer certificates at junior and senior levels to successful candidates from schools. Four Royal Commissions met between 1850 and 1868 to consider the education provided respectively by elementary, public and endowed schools and the universities; all four of their reports extolled the virtues of examinations. The rise in status of geography in the schools and colleges of Britain is closely linked with its growth in importance as an examinable subject.

Some idea of the content of the geography which was taught in school a hundred years ago can be gleaned from the questions set in some of the early Certificate examinations. The following specimens are taken from the *Report on Geographical Education* which was presented to the Council of the Royal Geographical Society in 1885 by J. Scott Keltie:

Cambridge Junior Local Certificate 1884
(1)   Name in order the chief capes on the east coast of England and Scotland between Dover and Aberdeen, and the counties in which they are situated.
(2)   With what industries are the following places specially connected and where are they situated: Burslem, Creuzot, Crewe, Droitwich, Lyons, Mobile, Monte Video, Odessa, Paisley, Rangoon?

Oxford Senior Local Certificate 1884
(1)   Give the chief tributaries of the Amazon and of the Obi. Illustrate by sketch maps.
(2)   Explain the terms – the Khamsin, delta, littoral, cañon, prairie, selva, sierra, pampa, estuary, tornado.

These few examples illustrate the fact that during the nineteenth century much of the geography studied in school consisted of learning by heart long lists of places and products, and a curious preoccupation with the coastal indentations of our islands gave rise to the derisory term 'capes and bays' geography for the conception of the subject which laid excessive emphasis upon rote-memory work. There was no dearth of textbooks which supported this concept; they were packed with information of an encyclopaedic nature about the countries of the world. One of the best-selling texts was the *School Geography*, first published in 1847, which went through sixty-three editions in the space of twenty-three years. Written by James Cornwell, the principal of Borough Road Training

College, it was full of lengthy exercises to test the memory, but there were neither maps nor photographs to relieve the monotony of the printed word. Another book with the same title was written by James Clyde; first issued in 1859, it had reached its twenty-second edition by 1883. Devoid of maps or illustrations, it concentrated on giving a plethora of facts and place-names to be committed to memory by its young readers. Yet the author stated in his preface that he had applied two tests to all that he had written: 'Is it examinable and is it rememberable?'

Although professional geographers have developed a more enlightened conception of their subject during the present century, laymen are still inclined to associate geography with the learning of place locations. This topic was aired in the correspondence columns of the *Guardian* not long ago, following the publication of a letter from a parent who complained that in spite of the high cost of his daughter's education at a girls' public (i.e. private) school, she did not know where Bacup was situated and she thought that the river Trent entered the sea at Liverpool. Reaction to this letter varied considerably, from the parent who reported a similar disappointment with his own daughter's schooling, to another who wondered if the position of Bacup was worth knowing anyway? A headmaster deplored the attempt to revive the outdated and discredited 'capes and bays' geography which was taught to him and to the parent who initiated this correspondence (a tacit recognition that the memorising of place-names in geographical teaching had continued well into the present century!); another correspondent was frankly envious of the young lady's ignorance, for whereas he knew exactly where he would be if he travelled a hundred kilometres north-east from his home-town, life to the girl who was hazy about the location of places must be full of surprises, with travel as a constantly exciting revelation of the unknown. The master of an Oxford college wrote to support the complaint of the parent who had initiated the correspondence, declaring that many of his honours students reading modern history had a bland ignorance of geographical knowledge of locations which left him amazed and irritated. He said that as a general rule the standard of geographical teaching was in inverse proportion to the reputation of the public school which his students had attended and he deplored the 'lack of atlas-mindedness' in the products of such eminent schools, whose ostentatious pride in their ignorance of place-locations seemed to stem from some kind of intellectual snobbishness. At about the same time that this correspondence was being conducted in the *Guardian*, two lecturers in different colleges of education gave tests to the geography students in their respective establishments which revealed widespread ignorance of the whereabouts of important places in the world.

It seems likely that in recent years many teachers who are anxious to make geography an interesting subject have rejected almost all the drill-work which, in moderate amounts, might be regarded as an integral part of the learning process. The vogue for teaching geography on a regional basis during the first half of the present century probably increased the number of places to be remembered, for the location of Buenos Aires learned in the first year gave no help in memorising the position of Bombay or Bergen in subsequent years. Any teacher who conscientiously attempts to give more attention than is currently fashionable to the identification of important features and locations which form the groundwork of geography faces the dilemma of selection, for no authoritative standards are laid down by the Department of Education and Science, by visiting inspectors or by the main examination boards. There might be a wide measure of agreement that 16-year-olds ought to know the geographical position and significance of, let us say, London, New York, Paris and Calcutta – but what about Carlisle, Casablanca or Cairns? A few years ago a correspondent to the *Times Educational Supplement* complained that in an Ordinary level GCE geography examination candidates were asked to mark the position on an outline map of Barmouth; 'Barmouth', he expostulated, 'with a population of only 2,310!'

In this matter every teacher is his own arbiter and stringent selection is necessary, for only a very small proportion of the places which are named in the textbook, the daily newspaper, or radio and television bulletins are worthy of being remembered with any precision. Some years ago I analysed the place-names of Australia which were mentioned in twenty-seven different regional textbooks intended for use in secondary schools by children aged 11 to 16. In these twenty-seven books there were altogether 711 different Australian place-names; only forty-one of these had what I called a high-frequency occurrence, that is, each one was found in more than three-quarters of the books. Eighty per cent of all the names were of low frequency, occurring in fewer than one-quarter of the texts, while 359 names – almost exactly half of the total number – were to be found in only one of the books, and thus had the lowest possible frequency.

Nineteenth-century geography in school gave undue emphasis to the pupil learning names by heart, parrot-fashion, without understanding the geographical significance of them, and it failed to discriminate between the important and the insignificant so that a child's head was stuffed with lists of undifferentiated names as in a gazetteer. Nevertheless, in rejecting the technique on these two counts, it would seem unwise to abandon altogether the principle of learning the significance (including the precise location) of a select number of outstanding places which receive attention during the course. There are various ways of reiterating the importance of these places, which need not occupy more than a few minutes of an occasional lesson. It could take the form of an oral quiz around the class as a prelude to the main theme; an outline map is sketched on the chalkboard or overhead projector, with the addition of dots or lines numbered 1 to 20 to represent towns, areas, minerals or specified physical features, the answers to be written down or delivered orally. A prepared passage of descriptive material with numbered blank spaces in the text can be duplicated and circulated for the class to complete. A simple crossword puzzle or a collection of anagrams can conceal the identity of places which have been mentioned in recent lessons. If the drill or revision can be conducted with a little of the light-hearted atmosphere of the television or radio quiz programme, so much the better! That which is tested need not be detested. I once conducted a weekly ten-minute test with a class of 11-year-olds, based on places which had been mentioned recently in news bulletins and newspapers. It began as a means of reinforcing the geographical location of places in the news, even though the news was not strictly geographical – it could be an assassination, earthquake, Test Match or royal visit. After a few weeks I allowed the pupil with the best score to compile the test for the following week, and by establishing the rule that no pupil could set the test more than once, even though he continued to score the highest mark, I was able to distribute the 'prize' to a different boy each week. It stimulated the study of newspapers in their homes and provided a light prelude to the more serious business of the Thursday lesson.

At the most elementary level, geographical knowledge merges imperceptibly into general knowledge. For some years before the Second World War selection for secondary education had involved the testing of primary school children at the age of 11, but this procedure assumed critical importance after the Education Act of 1944 had abolished the purchase of all places in maintained secondary schools. Henceforth the allocation of children to schools which were suited to their age, ability and aptitude became a delicate affair of teachers' assessments, record cards, and performance in standardised selection tests of English, arithmetic and verbal reasoning or 'intelligence'. Elementary geographical facts appeared in several of these intelligence test questions, as the following examples reveal:

A In each of the following questions all but one of the things are

alike in some way. Underline the *different* one:
(1)   York/Birmingham/Sussex/Manchester/Newcastle.
(2)   England/Ireland/London/Scotland/Wales.

B In each of the following questions there are TWO things which are like each other in some way but are different from the others in the question. Find the TWO that are most like each other in some way, and underline them:
(1)   Birmingham/England/Thames/Yorkshire/Newcastle/ Europe.
(2)   Wheat/meat/carrots/barley/fruit.

C Underline in the brackets the correct answer to each of the following:
(1)   Hill is to Mountain as Wood is to (tree/meadow/thicket/forest/river/valley).
(2)   Path is to Road as Stream is to (water/bank/mountain/river/sea).
(3)   July is to Summer as December is to (January/Christmas/winter/cold/snow/spring).
(4)   Man is to Bread as Sheep is to (wool/mutton/shepherd/lamb/grass/bleat).

The inference to be drawn from the examples labelled A and B is that a working knowledge of the various administrative units and larger cities in Britain was regarded as part of the mental equipment of the average 11-year-old by the person who devised the questions, an assumption which presumably had been confirmed by the pre-testing procedure. However, when Gustav Jahoda gave tests to children in Scottish primary schools to find out how far they understood the relationship between a city (Glasgow), the country in which that city was located (Scotland) and the connection between Scotland and the other units which together make up Britain (England, Wales), using a number of ingenious diagrams, he found that only half of the children aged 10 and 11 who came from a working-class neighbourhood had reached an adequate concept of these elementary space-relationships, although the children from middle-class homes scored higher marks on the same test.

With reference to the examples under C, a few years ago when public interest in the rights and wrongs of selection at 11-plus was at its peak, the *Guardian* newspaper published a leading article entitled 'Parents' guide to the 11-plus', which was being reprinted from an issue of *Where*?, the journal of the Advisory Centre for Education. This article described the function of selection tests and the various types in use by local education authorities. Verbal reasoning or

These Canadian lumberjacks are magnificent fellers; after a tiring day's work in the forests cutting timber they crawl wearily into their cabins and sleep like logs

intelligence tests were not only an important component of the battery of tests making up the '11-plus examination', but they also helped to determine a child's Intelligence Quotient (IQ). After stating that it takes about two years to produce a standardised test, because it has to be pre-tested on groups of children aged 11-plus to see whether it serves its purpose, and to eliminate items which are too easy or too hard for the average child of that age, the article quoted specimens of questions taken from tests administered in the past. One of these read as follows:

'Penguin is to Arctic as Monk is to (Church/ape/monastery/ abbot/nunnery).'

This prompted one reader to write to the editor of the *Guardian* with these comments:

'It is a pity that penguins do not live in the Arctic. If they did, parents might have more faith in the 11-plus examination. However, if a nunnery is poles apart from a monastery, then the answer to the question is obvious.'

Criticism of the extent to which intelligence tests measure the reasoning powers of the candidate has been voiced by John Wilson. In his opinion one weakness of these objective tests is that they do not take into account the reasoning by which the testee arrives at an answer, so he may gain points for giving the right answer even though his reasoning was incorrect, or he may have reached an incorrect alternative on rational grounds. In mathematics lessons the teacher usually tells his class to show their working, and not merely write down the bare answer. Moreover, the setters of intelligence tests often assume that the testee will be aware of certain unwritten conventions regarding the test question, for example, that no unnecessary information is included. Wilson quotes a question mentioned by H. J. Eysenck:

'Here are five towns. Which one is the "odd man out"? –
Panama, London, Duluth, Cambridge, Edsele.'

In this case the testee is expected to ignore geographical reasons for differences in the five towns (although in the examples given earlier under A, B and C the choice of correct answer depended upon geographical reasoning!) and to reach the correct answer by studying the letters in each name. According to the setter Cambridge is the right answer because it contains three different vowels, whereas all the other towns have but one vowel which is repeated two or three times. One could argue that Cambridge is also odd because it has nine letters to the six letters of the other four words, or that Panama is the odd one because it alone has a vowel alternating with a consonant throughout (all the others have two consonants juxtaposed). Moreover, Edsele could be considered exceptional in as much as it begins with a vowel while all the others begin with a consonant! But in these matters the compiler's decision is final ...

The reorganisation of Britain's educational system since 1965 has removed the sting of the 11-plus selection procedure in those areas where all children now proceed without test to a comprehensive secondary school. In these reorganised areas attention has been diverted to the tests which appear at the end of the secondary school course instead of at its beginning. Here the trend has been to diversify the form of the examination, in order to cater for a greater spread of ability among those about to leave school, whether at 16 or 18 years, to involve teachers more fully in marking and moderating procedures and to introduce objective tests in place of the traditional, highly subjective essay-type questions. The desire to be fair to all candidates and to eliminate variations in the standard of marking between different examiners has encouraged the introduction of multiple-choice and completion tests, which can now take one of several forms. The simplest type is where the stem consists of a question or an incomplete sentence, and the answer has to be chosen from five possible responses or options, only one of which is correct, the other possible choices being distractors. At the lowest level this is merely a test of the candidate's ability to recall the information learnt earlier, but more sophisticated types of multiple-choice, in which there may be more than one correct response among the four or five options, attempt to test the ability of the candidate to apply reasoning in reaching the correct answer. The stem can consist of a photograph, map, descriptive passage or table of statistics which has to be studied in order to arrive at the correct response or combination of responses, and the reasoning can be built into the question to eliminate or at least reduce guesswork. The chief criticism of the objective-type question is that it does not enable the candidate to exercise any literary ability in composing a stylish answer, so the essay-type question has not disappeared entirely from the examination scene.

It is customary for teachers to test pupils in Certificate years with questions taken from recent examination papers, but lower down the school the teacher can introduce more variety in the tests which he uses to keep his charges mentally alert. An essay is easy to set, whether as homework or classwork, but it is tedious to assess, and the number of young pupils who can sustain a reasonable literary style for two or three pages is very limited. Hence a useful alternative to the essay and one which is infinitely easier to mark is to supply a number of key-words or phrases, relating to the topic, and instruct the class to write an equivalent number of sentences so that each key-word is used once in a sentence to indicate its geographical significance. Thus in place of an essay on 'Coffee cultivation in Brazil', the following eight key-words could be supplied, with instructions to compose one sentence about each of them:

Fazenda; terra roxa; coffee berries; frost; Sao Paulo; subsistence crops; diversification; exports.

This technique permits the pupil to display any literary style he may possess and the teacher can rapidly assess the result by awarding 0, 1 or 2 marks for each sentence.

Some years ago Philip Vernon wrote a useful pamphlet for the Secondary Schools Examination Council in which he outlined the construction and special features of objective tests for the Certificate of Secondary Education, but it is well to bear in mind the distinction between tests which are conducted as part of the lesson sequence in class and examinations which take place after a series of lessons has been completed. The function of the latter is to grade candidates into pass or fail categories as fairly as possible, using their answers as a measure of their ability. On the other hand, tests which are administered in class should form an integral part of the learning process so that evaluation of the tests and the responses to them become a vital part of the dialogue between teacher and pupils, filling any gaps in the pupils' knowledge and clearing up any remaining doubts or misunderstandings about the topics under consideration. In an examination the tests are marked without taking into consideration the reasoning by which a candidate arrived at the answers, but in the classroom the teacher can discover why some pupils gave incorrect responses to certain questions and how far the wording of the items has stimulated the pupils to reason along the right lines towards the correct answers.

In recent years several books of multiple-choice tests have been published for classroom use. Some of these use only one type of test throughout the book, usually the kind with four or five options, only one of which is the correct response. Others, however, use a variety of tests involving reasoning as well as recall, and two examples of these publications may be mentioned. Ernest Clarke has edited two collections of *Objective and Completion Tests in O-Level Geography*, one on physical and general topics, the other on the British Isles, while W. E. Marsden has compiled two sets of *Multiple Choice and Structured Questions in Geography*, each with an introduction designed to show the vital feedback role which they can play in the classroom; one book deals with the British Isles and the other relates to Western Europe and world problems.

Many teachers like to supplement a book of tests with questions which they have constructed themselves around the topics covered during the past term or year. It is a lengthy process compiling objective-type questions but once assembled they can be stored and used repeatedly whenever the opportunity arises, and there is scope for more varied forms of presentation than is possible in a printed book. For example, twenty or thirty coloured pictures cut out from old geographical magazines or newspaper supplements, showing scenes or processes which have been studied during the term, are each pasted onto the upper half of a numbered piece of card; beneath the picture a question and five possible answers, lettered A to E, are written boldly with a felt pen, and one card is given to each pupil. These can be exchanged as soon as the pupil has recorded the card number and lettered answer on a separate sheet of paper, and

have the merit that each pupil can work at his own pace until the
time is up.

If several weeks have been occupied with the regional geography
of a specific country or region and the teacher has a number of slides
of that region which the class have not previously seen, a novel and
useful revision test can take the form of a projected slide show.
Beforehand, the teacher draws an outline map of the region, printing
different letters of the alphabet in place of the names of towns,
ports, mountain ranges, rivers, important commodities produced
such as wheat, fruits, sheep, tin, coal, and so on, making sure that
there is a letter on the location of each transparency. Having
arranged the slides in the order of projection, the teacher then writes
in a suitable space on the margin of the map a list of numbers to
match the number of slides to be shown. Against each number he
prints four different letters, one of which correctly locates the scene
of the projected slide while the other three are distractors. The map
with its completed list of numbers and letters is then duplicated and
one copy given to each pupil before the slides are projected. As each
slide is shown the teacher calls out its number and asks the class a
question, for example, 'Whereabouts is the cultivation of this crop
an important activity?'. Each pupil first decides the nature of the
crop, then studies the four possible locations and circles the chosen
answer. The wording of the questions can be geared to the abilities
of the class; thus for less able pupils the teacher might tell them the
name of the crop and then ask for its location on the map. Valuable
feedback results from a second showing of the slides when the
correct answers are given.

There seems to be no reason why an important examination should
always be utterly serious to be effective, so it was pleasing to observe
than a pun was used, by design, in a question set for the normally
sedate and decorous General Certificate of Education examination.
In 1975 the Ordinary level history paper (syllabus B) of the London
University Examinations Board included a multiple-choice question
which asked why Pope Pius IX was nicknamed Pio Nono. This
mystified a number of teachers until the history subject officer of the
examining board explained in a letter to the *Times Educational
Supplement* that the pun was a contemporary joke, printed in *Punch*
in January 1865, which had been converted into an examination
question 'to serve the additional purpose of adding a little variety
and humour to the examination paper'. Full marks to this particular
examiner! We can now look forward to the time when a touch of
humour will creep into a geography paper at the equivalent grade. It
may not have the candidates rolling in the aisles of the examination
hall but it will serve its purpose if it brings to their wan faces the

merest flicker of a wry smile, during their ordeal.

In common with several other subjects studied in school, geography contains a number of trifling yet fundamental and recurring details which need to be known with precision if the learner wishes to impress his teachers and examiners. These minor matters frequently consist of pairs of related terms which the novice is apt to confuse; east and west, for example, or latitude and longitude; the Tropics of Cancer and Capricorn; the precedence taken by eastings or northings in a six-figure grid reference; in the sphere of geomorphology there are anticlines and synclines, clints and grykes, dykes and sills, stalactites and stalagmites. Frequent usage enables these terms to become separately identifiable – although I have known young honours graduates in geography who confidently referred to the Tropic of Cancer as Capricorn, and confused east with west – but until acquaintance with these terms has ripened into deep understanding, any mnemonic which may help to harness these wayward expressions is to be welcomed. Mental props of this nature are common to many subjects of study; the historian uses them to recall alliances made during the various wars of European history, or to place in chronological order the ruling houses of Britain from the Normans onward; the student of foreign languages employs them to remember irregular plural forms, the budding nurse or anatomist devises complex formulae for memorising the groups of bones in the body, while many people never get beyond the stage of reciting 'Thirty days hath September . . . ' in order to recall the number of days in July. Yet writers of textbooks and manuals of teaching techniques are curiously reluctant to recommend the use of mnemonics. Perhaps they fear that such action might be construed as tacit approval of learning facts by heart instead of by understanding, a concept of geography which is now rightly discredited and discarded. Brayshaw, the headmaster of Keighley Grammar School in the middle years of the nineteenth century, made his pupils learn by heart hundreds of rhymes and facts which he published as *Metrical Mnemonics* in 1849. Nowadays we recognise that memorising may actually impede understanding, so that a mnemonic is useful only as an aid to comprehension, it is not an end in itself and should be discarded as soon as the facts are thoroughly understood. During my visits to students on teaching practice I have occasionally had to devise a formula to remind me of the successive streets to follow in order to get to a particular school which I was visiting for the first time, and this mnemonic was used for one or two subsequent visits until the route had become familiar to me. There might then be an interval of several years before I had occasion to visit that particular school again, but invariably I could at once recall *visually* the route to take, while the mnemonic which I had devised for the original visit and the names of the streets involved, had been completely forgotten! It is only the learner who has need of mnemonics; once he has acquired a thorough understanding of his subject he relies on habit or reasoning instead of memory.

The following collection of memory aids, assembled over the years, is presented in something like alphabetical order, pairs of associated terms being listed under the first name. (They are not so numerous that a cross-reference to the second item in a pair is necessary.)

GEO-MNEMONICS, OR DEVICES TO 'GEOG' THE MEMORY

Anticline and Syncline
Which one is the downfold?

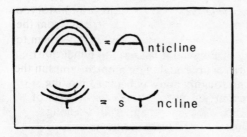

Figure 12 *Anticline and syncline*

Atmospheric Pressure
Winds blow from HIGH to LOW.
In the northern hemisphere if you stand with your back to the wind, the *L*ow pressure is on your *L*eft.
(And therefore the *HIGH* pressure is on your *RIGHT*.)

Australian rainfall boomerangs (adapted from T. Pickles, *The Southern Continents*)
The northern boomerang includes areas with a pronounced summer maximum of rain, the southern boomerang covers the parts of Australia with a marked winter maximum. (Tasmania and the neighbourhood of Sydney have roughly equal parts of rain in the summer and winter halves of the year, so there is no marked dry season there.) See Figure 13, overleaf.

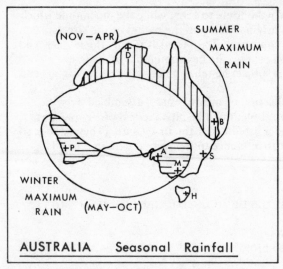

Figure 13 *Australia: rainfall boomerangs*

Belgium: ABC cities
When drawing a sketch map of Belgium it is useful to remember that
Antwerp, Brussels and Charleroi are roughly on a north–south line,
with the capital Brussels lying roughly midway between the western
and eastern borders of the country.

Clints and grykes
Which are the blocks and which are the fissures?
If your foot falls into the fissure you shout
'O grykey!'

Common Market Countries (European Economic Community)
*L*ady *G*odiva *I*s *D*isplaying *H*er *B*eautiful *B*ody *I*n *F*ull.
(Luxembourg, Germany (West), Italy, Denmark, Holland, Belgium,
Britain, Ireland, France.)
The purists who wish to refer to Netherlands in place of Holland can
substitute 'Nude' for 'Her' as the fifth word!

Californian Current
Is it warm or cool?
Cool Californian Current – C C C (Si, si, si, there was a strong
Spanish influence in California). If it is remembered that it is cool
because it is flowing south from northern waters towards warmer
tropical waters it establishes the circulation of water in the North

Pacific Ocean. (In the northern hemisphere, Current Circulation is Clockwise.)

Demersal and Pelagic Fish
Which kind feed on the seabed?
Think of fish-pond. P-on (i.e. above) -D.
P = *P*elagic, near the to*P*
o
n
D = *D*emersal, near the seabe*D*.

Dyke and Sill
Which type of igneous intrusion is horizontal?

Figure 14 *Dyke and sill*

Figure 15 *West and east*

East and West
It is surprising how many find difficulty in distinguishing between these two cardinal points of the compass; there is much less confusion between north and south, possibly because the phrases 'up north' and 'down south' help to identify them. Younger children can remember the four main points *in clockwise order* by a nonsense phrase:

(1)   Never Eat Shredded Wheat
      (North East South   West)

(2)   A better alternative is to visualise the map of England and
      Wales (Figure 15).

Wales is to the West of England on the East.

Geological Sequence of Sedimentary Rocks
Camels Often Sit Down Carefully.
Perhaps Their Joints Creak?
Early Oiling Might Prevent Permanent Rheumatism.
(Cambrian Ordovician Silurian Devonian Carboniferous
Permian Triassic Jurassic Cretaceous
Eocene Oligocene Miocene Pliocene Pleistocene Recent)
(Quoted in *A Dictionary of Mnemonics*, Eyre Methuen, 1972, p. 24.)

Global Position
The Equator runs through the mouth of the Amazon River in South
America, the northern shores of Lake Victoria in East Africa, the
middle of Sumatra and Borneo (Kalimantan) islands in South-East
Asia.
    The Tropic of Cancer runs through the southern tip of the
Mexican peninsula of Lower California in North America and the
Sahara Desert in Africa, close to Karachi, Calcutta and Canton in
Asia and to Honolulu in the Hawaiian Islands in the Pacific Ocean.
    The Tropic of Capricorn runs through Antofagasta and Sao Paulo
in South America, the Kalahari Desert in South Africa and
Rockhampton in Australia.
    Cairo in Egypt is approximately 30°N and 30°E while New
Orleans is roughly 30°N and 90°W. These and other useful
approximations can be discovered by anyone who cares to consult an
elementary atlas or a globe.

Great Lakes of North America
Going downstream, i.e. from west to east, from the interior to the
River St Lawrence:
(1)   Some Men Hate Eating Onions.
(2)   Some Mothers Have Energetic Offspring.
(Superior, Michigan, Huron, Erie, Ontario).

Grid References
The point of origin of the reference system for British maps is off the
south-west tip of Cornwall, so the sequence of readings is:

(1) Eastings before Northings.
     (E is before N in the alphabet)

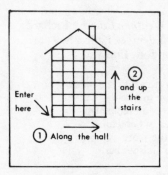

Figure 16 *Eastings and northings*

(2) With young children the grid pattern can be made to resemble a
     house and the rule is:
     Along the hall (eastings) and up the stairs (northings).

International Date Line
Going west (across the IDL) a day 'goes west', i.e. it is struck off the
calendar.

Latitude and Longitude
In a gazetteer the convention is to quote the latitude of a place first,
followed by the longitude.
(1) LAT. before LONG. i.e. in alphabetical order.
(2) On a world map drawn on a cylindrical projection such as
     Mercator's,
     L*A*TITUDE lines run *A*CROSS the map and
     L*O*NGITUDE lines run D*O*WN the map.
(3) But since this is not true of all projections a better mnemonic is
     L*A*TITUDE lines run *E*AST to WEST and
     L*O*NGITUDE lines run N*O*RTH to SOUTH.

Local Time Differences
If you go *EAST* the new local time will be *FAST*, i.e. ahead of your
original time.
     If you go *WEST* the new local time will be *SLOW*, i.e. behind
your original time.
     Local time alters ONE HOUR for every FIFTEEN DEGREES of

LONGITUDE, since the earth turns through 360° of longitude every twenty-four hours.

London monthly temperatures

This ingenious rhyme, which appears in *Weather Lore* by Richard Inwards, gives the average temperature in degrees Fahrenheit for each month of the year in the area of London, England:

> Round the whole of the year fifty stands as the mean.
> For July and for August we add on thirteen:
> Put four on for May, ten for June, and remember
> To allow eight degrees for the heat of September:
> October improves one degree on the year,   -
> But the list of the warmer months finishes here.
>
> Cold January's down by eleven degrees;
> Next, December and February, ten off for these;
> Make it seven for March and November, and two
> For the fickle month April. And that sees us through.

Hence we get, in degrees Fahrenheit:

J	F	M	A	M	J	J	A	S	O	N	D
39	40	43	48	54	60	63	63	58	51	43	40

However, since we now record temperatures on the Celsius scale, the above monthly figures read as follows in degrees Centigrade:

J	F	M	A	M	J	J	A	S	O	N	D
3·9	4·4	6·1	8·9	12·2	15·6	17·2	17·2	14·4	10·6	6·1	4·4

The decimal fractions make it impossible to update the rhyme merely by changing from Fahrenheit to Centigrade, so I have had to make a free translation in order to preserve the rhyming couplets. Unfortunately the mental arithmetic becomes more involved, so the modern version is probably less useful than the original jingle:

> The mean for the year is ten C but affix
> Two-point-two on for May and for June five-point-six:
> July, August rise seven-point-two and remember
> To add four-point-four for the heat of September:
> October improves nought-point-six on the mean
> And the list of the warmer months now can be seen.
>
> Cold January's down by six-point-one degrees;
> Next, December and Feb., five-point-six off for these;
> Three-point-nine off for March and Novem.; one-point-one
> Is deducted for April. And then we have done.

Mediterranean-Type Climate
Warm Wet Winters With Westerly Winds and Hot Dry Summers.

Northern Ireland
The initial letters of the six counties of Northern Ireland spell FAT
LAD
(Fermanagh, Armagh, Tyrone, Londonderry, Antrim, Down).

Rhine Gorge
Between the towns of Bingen and Bonn the river Rhine flows
through a plateau of Hercynian rocks in a narrow gorge.

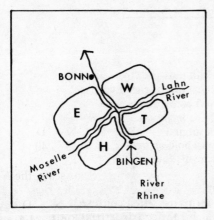

Figure 17 *The Rhine Gorge*

The positions of these towns can be remembered by the phrase

> From Bingen to Bonn
> The Rhine flows on.

The Hercynian plateau is cut into four blocks by the Rhine and two
tributaries, the Moselle on the left bank and the Lahn on the right;
these blocks in alphabetical order anti-clockwise from Bonn are:

Eifel, Hunsruck, Taunus and Westerwald.

South Wales coalfield
The main producing areas for Anthracite, Steam and Household
coals are roughly in the west, central and eastern parts of the field
respectively, thus spelling the word ASH. See Figure 18 overleaf.

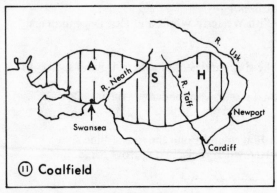

Figure 18 *The South Wales coalfield*

Stalactites and Stalagmites
(1)   Stala*C*tites grow from the *C*eiling of the cave.
       Stala*G*mites grow from the *G*round of the cave.
(2)   'mites' grow up, 'tites' (tights) come down.
(3)   A stalag*mite* you just *might* see
                               Growing from the ground
                               But a stalac*tite* must hold on *tight*
                               To the ceiling where it's found.

Tropics of Cancer and Capricorn
As with east and west, these two terms are often confused.
(1)   Cancer (six letters) cuts through Mexico (six letters) in the
       northern hemisphere.
       Capricorn (nine letters) cuts through Australia (nine letters) in
       the southern hemisphere.
(2)   Cancer of the chest i.e. upper part of the body, northern
       hemisphere.
       Corns on your feet, i.e. lower extremity, southern hemisphere.

Yorkshire rivers
The right-bank tributaries of the Yorkshire Ouse between the Tees
and the Trent:
*S*heffield *U*nited *N*ever *W*in *A*ny *C*ups, *D*ad.
(Swale, Ure, Nidd, Wharfe, Aire, Calder, Don.)
A map of these rivers appears in several textbooks to illustrate river-
capture.

Mnemonics are like funny stories, they appeal to some but not to
others, and much of their effectiveness hangs on the mode of

presentation. Thus a mnemonic which is a play upon the name of
one of the pupils will probably be remembered by the members of
that class, whereas it may fail to impress if presented to a different
group. In like manner, local references have a stronger appeal – the
last one in the above list is popular in South Yorkshire because of the
interest in the fortunes of the football team quoted – it does not seem
to matter whether the phrase is historically accurate or not! A master
of my acquaintance who was a keen follower of cricket used to help
his boys to remember the gap towns in the North Downs by reference
to an eminent cricketer of a bygone age, Dr Grace:

*W*ey *G*ap, *G*uildford; *M*ole gap, *D*orking
W. G. Grace, MD.

Care must be taken to ensure that a mnemonic relating to details
which are subject to alteration does not become outdated with the
passage of time. Statistics of population, economic production,
administrative boundaries and even place-names can alter alarmingly
within a comparatively short period, so that an acronym formed
from the names of the leading countries for the production or export
of a certain commodity may need revision more than once during a
teacher's career. Changes in the standard system of measurement can
play havoc with long-established mnemonics. Several generations of
budding geographers stored in their minds a potted summary of
seasonal temperature conditions over the British Isles by memorising
the routes taken by the mean monthly sea-level isotherms of 40°
Fahrenheit for January and 60° for July, which intersected to divide
the British Isles into four quadrants. But all that has now been
changed; Fahrenheit has given way to Centigrade and it is not merely
a matter of altering the values of the isotherms to 4·4°C for January
and 15·6° for July, for the Meteorological Office has used revised
data to redraw these isotherms, which now wriggle sinuously across
the map in a kinky manner quite unlike their former gentle wave-like
motion. In consequence it matters not whether the pupil
superimposes the 5° or 6° Centigrade isotherm for January upon the
15° or 16° isotherm for July, he will not get the clear-cut pattern of
quadrants which was formerly obtained. Moreover, he now has to
contemplate the rainfall for representative areas of Britain in terms
of hundreds of millimetres instead of a score or so of inches. In
truth, conversion to metric units is confounding many mnemonics,
and the best memory-aids are those which relate to fundamental,
unalterable facts of geography such as the cardinal points of the
compass.

REFERENCES

T. Brayshaw, *Metrical Mnemonics applied to Geography, Astronomy and Chronology*, etc. (London, Simpkin Marshall, 1849).

Ernest Clarke (ed.), *Objective and Completion Tests in O-Level Geography – Physical and General Geography* (London, John Murray, 1971); *The British Isles* (London, John Murray, 1975).

J. Clyde, *School Geography* (London, Constable, 1859).

J. Cornwell, *School Geography* (London, Simpkin Marshall, 1847).

R. Inwards, *Weather Lore*, rev. E. L. Hawke (London, Royal Meteorological Society, 1950).

G. Jahoda, 'The development of children's ideas about country and nationality', *British Journal of Educational Psychology*, vol. 33, 1963, pp. 47–60.

L. J. Jay, 'Significant place-names in school geography', *Geography*, vol. 39, 1954, pp. 28–32.

J. S. Keltie, 'Geographical education', *Royal Geographical Society Supplementary Papers*, Vol. 1, 1886, pp. 538, 540.

W. E. Marsden, *Multiple Choice and Structured Questions in Geography – British Isles* (Edinburgh, Oliver & Boyd, 1975); *Western Europe and World Problems* (Edinburgh, Oliver & Boyd, 1975).

P. Vernon, *The Certificate of Secondary Education: An Introduction to Objective-Type Examinations*, SSEC Examinations Bulletin No. 4 (London, HMSO, 1964).

Chapter 6

Travelling for the Fun of It

Readers of the stories about Winnie-the-Pooh by A. A. Milne will
recall the occasion when Christopher Robin took the Bear and
Rabbit and his other friends on what Pooh called an Expotition to
discover the North Pole. The adventure ended when Roo, who had
fallen into a stream, was rescued by grasping a long stick which
Pooh had found nearby. Before the travellers turned back for home
a notice was affixed to the pole to certify that Pooh had discovered
it.

Long before children begin the formal study of geography in
school they are fascinated by stories of travel and discovery. At first
these may be imaginary journeys made by a make-believe prince who
rescues a beautiful damsel in distress and carries her off to his castle,
or they may be the equally fictitious but far more credible stories
about the search for treasure on islands in faraway tropical seas.
From the time they can walk children savour the thrill of personal
exploration of the unknown; it may be the first visit to the house of a
friend or relative, with its unfamiliar furniture and corridors; a tour
of a building site when the workmen have gone home, with pitfalls
galore for the unwary and the dare of walking the plank from one
roofless room to the next; or the excitement of finding the quickest
route to the beach on first arriving at the summer holiday resort. To
the very young almost every journey is an adventure for so much of
the surrounding world is strange and full of wonder. What a pity
that formal geography lessons so rarely capture the atmosphere of
excitement which attaches to one of the early explorations of the
neighbourhood made by a venturesome child.

Travel and exploration have always constituted a respectable
element of geography, more especially so in the years before it
became established as a university discipline. It was the initiative of
Sir Joseph Banks, a wealthy botanist who had travelled with James
Cook across the Pacific and who was president of the Royal Society
for forty-three consecutive years, which led to the formation of the
Africa Association in 1788 to promote the exploration of that
continent, and it was this Association which engaged Mungo Park,
one of the first of the modern explorers to gain wide popularity with
the public, to undertake his travels in West Africa. At the end of the

Napoleonic Wars exploration and continental travel became a popular activity for demobilised officers of the army and navy, and this led in 1819 to the formation of a Travellers' Club in London; it was a condition of membership that every applicant should have travelled beyond the British Isles for at least 800 km in a direct line from London, and very soon there were close on 500 members claiming to have this qualification. (This club is still in existence, with its headquarters in Pall Mall and a membership exceeding 1,000.) In 1826 one of the original members, Captain Arthur de Capell Brooke, felt that the Travellers' Club was too large for members to get to know each other at meetings, so he formed a breakaway group which became known as the Raleigh Club; designed principally as a dining club, its membership was limited to fifty persons who between them had travelled in every quarter of the globe. Thirteen men attended the first dinner, at which reindeer venison from Spitzbergen, cloud berries from Lapland and a jar of Swedish brandy, all donated by Captain Brooke, formed part of the menu.

At a meeting of the Raleigh Club in 1830 the desirability of creating a society for the promotion and diffusion of geographical knowledge was discussed at great length, and this led to the foundation of the Royal Geographical Society. Patronised by royalty and supported by many eminent and affluent men, the society enjoyed great prestige during the reign of Queen Victoria, and it was jestingly said that exploration meant the first discovery of new land by a white man, preferably an Englishman, and only really authentic if the venture had been sponsored by the Royal Geographical Society. Nevertheless it should be recognised that the society was most influential in its encouragement and financial support of many successful expeditions, and most of the discoveries which filled in blank spaces on the world map since 1830 have been described at length in the publications of the Royal Geographical Society. The Raleigh Club, which from the start had been closely identified with the society, was reconstituted as the Geographical Club in 1854 and under this name it still continues to flourish as a dining club for a select number of Fellows – so select, in fact, that not until 1972 were Lady Fellows of the society eligible for admission as members of the club!

During the nineteenth century the headquarters of the Royal Geographical Society became a popular rendezvous in London for men of substantial means with a taste for travel and adventure. Typical of these was Douglas Freshfield, a wealthy Victorian gentleman of ample means and leisure. As a child his summer holidays were spent with his parents visiting remote parts of the Alpine mountains, and he climbed Mont Blanc while still a boy at Eton. After graduating in law and history from Oxford he travelled

widely in Egypt and the Middle East. He climbed many peaks in the
Caucasus at a time when the character of that range was unknown to
most Europeans, and the two volumes he wrote on his explorations
of this area contained maps which were used by climbers as the best
available for the next forty years. Freshfield realised more keenly
than most of his contemporaries that travel and discovery formed
only one part, but not the whole, of geography, and he strove to
secure a firmer place for the subject in our educational system. He
persuaded the Council of the Royal Geographical Society to
subsidise the appointment of lecturers in geography at the
universities of Oxford and Cambridge and this, in time, led to a
supply of qualified geography teachers in secondary schools. In the
1890s there was much heated argument within the society which
spilled over into the correspondence columns of *The Times* and the
pages of *Punch* on the question of whether women should be
admitted as Fellows of the society. The vacillating policy of the
council over this matter so annoyed Freshfield that he resigned his
post as one of its honorary secretaries in 1893. He had a flair for
writing witty epigrams and the following example demonstrated his
support for the admission of ladies to membership of the society:

> The question our dissentients bellow
> Is 'Can a lady be a Fellow?'
> That, Sirs, will be no question when
> Our Fellows are all gentlemen.

In this same year the Geographical Association was formed with
the aim of furthering the knowledge and teaching of geography in
schools and other institutions. From the start it admitted women as
members with the same rights as men, and it was therefore most
fitting that the gallant English gentleman, Douglas Freshfield, should
be elected the first president of the association in 1897, a post to
which he was re-elected every year until 1911.

Freshfield was an accomplished scholar and writer, who was
responsible for starting the Royal Geographical Society's collection
of photographs and for introducing the lantern to provide pictorial
illustration for evening lectures, despite opposition from some
Fellows who thought he was debasing the standards of the society's
gatherings. It was at one of these illustrated evening lectures that
members were treated unexpectedly to the first moving picture ever
seen on the society's screen. A house-fly landed on the surface of a
projected slide; the screen was positioned above the head of the
lecturer who, unaware of the intruder, told his audience that they
were witnessing a particularly savage specimen of big game being

hunted. He failed to understand why each reference to the beast sent his audience into convulsions of laughter until he looked up at the screen and saw the monstrous shadow of the fly darting to and fro across the landscape pursued by a huge pole which was the shadow of a needle being used by the operator in a desperate attempt to remove the 'foreign body'. This anecdote is told in *The Record of the Royal Geographical Society 1830–1930*, written by Hugh Robert Mill, which gives many biographical details about Douglas Freshfield.

From 1815 to 1914 exploration by Europeans was largely directed to areas beyond their own continent; within Europe travellers directed their attention upwards rather than outwards to develop the rich man's sport of mountaineering, with Switzerland as a popular focus. Around the turn of the century much interest centred upon the Polar regions; Fridtjof Nansen made the first crossing of the Greenland ice-cap on skis in 1888 and five years later he deliberately manoeuvred his ship *Fram* to become trapped in the Arctic ice to test his theory concerning circum-polar currents. This same vessel was later loaned to a fellow Norwegian, Roald Amundsen, who used it to approach the South Pole which he reached five weeks ahead of Captain Scott and a British team.

A new-style explorer emerged during the years between the two world wars who used his youthfulness and private resources to travel for the fun of it in distant places with no pretence of conducting a scientific expedition. The experiences of these cheerful wanderers were often recorded in books which underplayed the dangerous situations and conditions they encountered, in sharp contrast to the ponderous heroic style of writing of an older school of explorers. Representative of these new young men was Peter Fleming, educated at Eton and Oxford, who at the age of 25 went to search for the missing Colonel Fawcett in the interior of Brazil.

The amusing and light-hearted account which he wrote about his experiences in South America was published in 1933 under the title *Brazilian Adventure* and achieved instant success. In one of its chapters he took to task the old men of his day who bewailed the absence of adventurous spirit in modern youth. He pointed out that for the Elizabethan explorers in the sixteenth century every other landfall meant a new colonial possession; all that was needed in those days was an inquiring turn of mind and a profound contempt for scurvy and Spaniards. In the 1930s, however, most of the land masses had been 'discovered' and scientific experts were consolidating the gains made by swash-buckling amateurs; in Darien today one needs not only a pair of eagle eyes, but a theodolite as well.

Fleming wrote disparagingly of those who attract public attention by performing some improbable and useless action such as driving a car in reverse along the Great Wall of China, or becoming the 'First Girl Mother to Swim Twice Round the Isle of Man'. He deplored feats which belittled the achievements of pioneers who had been the first to traverse a particular desert or sail down a river from source to mouth by performing the same journey in a shorter time, or by undertaking it on foot instead of on horseback. 'Statistical eye-wiping' he called it, and strangely enough in recent years there has been a recrudescence of this activity, prompted in no small measure by the publishing success of the *Guinness Book of Records*. First issued in October 1955, this popular compilation has now become an annual publication, and one suspects that many an eccentric feat of endurance is nowadays undertaken in the express hope that it will be accorded a mention in the next edition of the *Book of Records*. But, as Fleming observed, such feats bear about as much relation to adventure as a giant gooseberry does to agriculture.

The social and economic changes of the postwar years altered the conditions for travel and adventure, presenting greater opportunities to young people of modest means. The increase in the number of owners of small cars extended the scope of their weekend activities, while new techniques increased the popularity of recreations such as rock-climbing in Britain and abroad, producing mountaineers of the calibre of Joe Brown, a Manchester plumber who began his climbing on the gritstone edges of the Peak District, using his mother's clothes line for rope. Caving and pot-holing provided outlets – or should it be inlets? – for weekend adventurers at a comparatively low cost, extending the scope of Mountain Rescue teams who now scale depths as well as heights. Altitude is a key factor in another sport which has grown in popularity in recent years, for new gliding clubs have sprung up in all parts of Britain; many of them utilise small airfields which were created during the last war but had since fallen into disuse and neglect. Geographers find this sport particularly satisfying, for the patterns of landforms and human occupation are vividly displayed to the observer who is gliding a few hundred metres above the countryside, while the study of local atmospheric circulation takes on a new significance in the quest for thermals. The inland waterways of Britain, both natural and man-made, are another focus for renewed activity in recent decades. Groups of eager volunteers spend their weekends clearing the débris from neglected canals so that these can once again become navigable for narrowboats and pleasure craft. Educational inland cruises for parties of sixth-formers, scouts, guides or youth club members provide an enjoyable and novel means of observing landforms and life in urban or rural settings, with tunnels and locks offering an exciting way of negotiating changes of gradient. New techniques of building small boats, combined with the increased accessibility of lakes, reservoirs and coastal waters to town-dwellers made possible by the car and minibus, have together increased the number of people who can now afford to go sailing. One form of exploration since the last war which has had a particular fascination for British adventurers is the long-distance voyage in a small boat, made either single-handed or by a small crew, revealing secrets about oceanic travel which had not previously been apparent to those voyaging in larger vessels. In 1947 a Norwegian anthropologist, Thor Heyerdahl, assembled a crew of five volunteers of various nationalities, supervised the construction in Peru of a raft made from balsa logs cut in the forests of Ecuador, and drifted on it for 100 days westwards across the Pacific Ocean before it broke up on the coral reef of Raroia. He made this voyage to prove that it was possible for people in prehistoric times to have migrated from South America to Polynesia using similar rafts made of balsa wood. A similar motive impelled Tim Severin and five companions to sail from Ireland to North America in an 11-metre open curragh made of oxhides. He modelled his boat on the specifications given in a mediaeval Latin manuscript known as the *Navigatio* of St Brendan, which described a voyage made by this Irish saint in a leather boat to the 'Promised Land' by way of islands in the North Atlantic, many years before the Norsemen reached Labrador. Severin and his crew sailed from southern Ireland in May 1976 and reached Iceland sixty days later. They wintered there and resumed their voyage the following May, making landfall in Newfoundland on 26 June 1977, thereby proving that it was possible for Irish seamen to have 'discovered' America during the Dark Ages.

In the last few decades solo voyages of great length have become fashionable exploits. For example, in 1952 a French doctor, Alain Bombard, crossed the Atlantic in a rubber dinghy, taking neither food nor water on board and surviving on plankton and fluids extracted from fish caught during the voyage. Sir Francis Chichester first achieved fame when he flew solo in a single-engined aeroplane from England to Australia; he was in his sixties when he set off alone in his yacht *Gipsy Moth IV* to circumnavigate the globe. In April 1969 Robin Knox-Johnston sailed into Falmouth harbour in his 10-metre ketch *Suhaili* after having lived in it for 313 consecutive days during a non-stop voyage round the world, the first person known to have completed such a journey single-handed without putting in at any port en route.

Every teacher should be alert to capture the excitement of travel and discovery which is latent in children at certain periods in their schooling. J. A. Morris once found himself facing a class of 11-year-olds for a course of lessons to occupy one term on the regional geography of South America. His knowledge of the subject-matter being on his own admission too scanty to extend over thirty lessons, he conceived the idea of an exploratory tour round the continent during which one of the boys in the form was killed off each lesson in a manner appropriately geographical and personal. Thus one sleepy boy was blown off their 'ship' as it rounded Cape Horn in a gale, another boy, noted for his large appetite, was eaten by a jaguar in the depths of Amazonia, while the big-head of the form fell victim to the savage tribesmen living in the interior of Ecuador who shrink the heads of their captives. The boys loved this treatment and clamoured to be liquidated. Years later, when they had grown to manhood, they would introduce themselves to their former geography master if they encountered him in the streets of London by reminding him of the way in which he had 'disposed' of them during their conducted tour of South America. Morris had clearly chosen the right manner and moment to exploit the love of adventure and travel with this particular group of boys. His treatment may not have resulted in the transmission of much formal geography for one term, but he probably established a rapport with his class which subsequently facilitated the study of more serious topics.

Scientific accounts of recent exploratory journeys continue to fill many pages of the *Geographical Journal*. These, however, are scarcely calculated to enthuse the budding geographer who is more likely to be attracted by the colourful descriptions of travel contained in the *National Geographic Magazine*, which also presents more formal topics in an attractive style. Nevertheless, the most vivid impact is provided nowadays by the programmes on colour television of films made during recent journeys of exploration and adventure, which are vastly superior in technique and presentation to the formalised travelogues made for the cinema screen in years past. There is little doubt that many people have been stimulated to read a travel book after having had their interest aroused by the condensed visual presentation of the contents in a television programme.

During the Depression of the 1930s few teachers in maintained schools had travelled far beyond the shores of their own island, for continental travel was a comparative luxury before the advent of package tours and air charter flights, while the rigid sequence of formal educational certificates acquired in a progression from school to college or university and then back to school as a qualified teacher presented few opportunities for an adventurous young person to spend a year abroad before starting upon a professional career. The enforced movements of personnel in wartime, however, gave unexpected experience of distant lands to many serving men and women who entered upon or resumed a career in teaching when they were demobilised after the war. Those who were teachers of geography could then convey at first hand to their pupils personal impressions of the scenery, climatic conditions and the way of life of the inhabitants of countries remote from the homeland. Greater flexibility in the educational requirements for teacher training in recent years has enlarged the opportunities for foreign travel, and many young persons elect to spend a year or more on voluntary service overseas, or else obtain temporary jobs in North America during the vacations, travelling at cheap student rates, before commencing to teach. Hitch-hiking has become a common practice among the youth of many countries and the modern 'back-packer' in jeans can be found in places as widely separated as California, Cornwall or Katmandu.

Children of school age also tend to be more widely travelled than their counterparts of thirty years ago. The rising standard of living has permitted more and more workers to take their families to Spain, Italy, Greece or islands in the Mediterranean for an annual holiday, or to pay for their children to go on an educational cruise in a liner specially converted to this use, while organised school journeys to many European countries, in winter and summer, have become an institution in many schools. In brief, both for pupils and teachers, foreign travel is playing a more significant role in the acquisition of geographical knowledge and understanding than it did a generation ago. Outside the independent school system it was once a rare event to come across a geography teacher who had lived for a year beyond the borders of Britain, and even more unusual to find a pupil who had done this, but nowadays many geographers have an impressive experience of foreign countries while in certain towns classes are likely to contain a large number of immigrant children whose parents come from far-off lands.

Whenever it is relevant to the subject of the lesson, pupils should be encouraged to share with the rest of the class their personal experiences of travel, whether in the homeland or overseas. A holiday visit to Iceland, Switzerland or the south of France may provide a verbal description of the Mistral, transhumance, valley glaciers or an active volcano which conveys detail not evident in the formal version tendered by the teacher or textbook, while even the mundane study of wheat cultivation in eastern England can be enlivened if one of the more articulate pupils is persuaded to describe the activities at her uncle's farm near Norwich during a holiday at harvest-time. It may well be necessary to edit these juvenile reports.

A package tour abroad may have taken the child to selected places catering for the tourist traffic where the appearance and activities of the inhabitants is not truly representative of the majority of the population. Moreover, the weather experienced during one fortnight on the Continent may have been atypical, perhaps unusually wet or cold for the season, failing to comply with the trite phrases or statistical monthly averages which are the conventional geographical shorthand employed to summarise the climate. Winters in the Mediterranean are not always warm and wet, nor are the summers always hot and dry. It is scarcely necessary to add that teachers should also describe to the class any incidents of their own travels which add colour and depth to the more prosaic passages of the textbook.

She doesn't pay much attention in my course on the historical geography of Britain – she thinks the Celtic fringe is a new hairstyle

The geographer who elects to travel in distant lands is unlike ordinary mortals on the move because he already has a shrewd idea of what he is going to see before he gets there, and his sources of information are usually free from the bias which colours the glossy, persuasive booklets put out by travel agencies and publicity departments. Yet few geographers are deterred from travelling by the thought that they already know in broad terms what is around the next corner, for they realise that the joy of discovery can apply to trivial details just as much as to the fundamental facts. Moreover, there is satisfaction in being able to confirm or correct for yourself some item which hitherto you had accepted from others. Some years ago I made a tour of the western half of the United States, accompanied by my wife, son and daughter; we planned to see as much as possible of the varied landscapes between the Midwest and the Pacific Ocean during the seven weeks available to me in between my lecturing commitments in America before we returned to Britain at the end of a year abroad. Tourism and recreation have recently become respectable branches of geographical study, so I make no apology for offering some personal observations here. My intention is to relate minor incidents and experiences of the kind which rarely receive mention in the orthodox textbook. They may be trivial or superficial and are certainly not to be compared with the stirring journeys made by the modern adventurers named earlier in the chapter. Yet they are perhaps characteristic of the unspectacular travels made by a vast number of ordinary folk at the present time, and it is personal experiences of this calibre, exchanged in the classroom between teacher and pupil, which can illuminate many a geography lesson.

We proposed to alternate motel accommodation with nights spent under canvas on camp-sites, having been loaned a tent and sleeping bags. When these items along with four small suitcases – one for each member of the family – had been stowed away in the boot of the seven-year-old Chevrolet car which I had bought the previous winter, we headed west out of Michigan along Highway 94 on a hot sunny morning in June. A week later we were camping in Aspen Glen at a height of 2,400 m among the scented pine-forests of the Rocky Mountain National Park. One afternoon we drove over to the Moraine Park Visitor Centre, built of logs and stone, where the geological history, fauna and flora of the park were attractively presented by means of maps, rock specimens, colour photographs and three-dimensional models. The entrance to the centre faced the low wooded ridge of the south lateral moraine left behind by the Big Thompson Glacier; beyond the ridge in the distance rose the serrated crest of the Front Range of the Rockies, dominated at the southern end by the 4,343 m of Longs Peak, the highest point in the national park. It was here that we encountered our first American nature trail, which looped around the hillside behind the visitor centre. At that time nature trails in Britain were only just beginning to appear, so we were interested to see what had been made of them in America's national parks. We put fifteen cents in a box shaped like a reading-desk and helped ourselves to one of a pile of trail-guides before starting our forty-minute walk along a clearly marked footpath. At intervals along the route a numbered marker indicated the presence nearby of some feature which was described and illustrated in the sixteen-page booklet; it might be the burrow of a

Wyoming ground squirrel, a bush of the black chokeberry, a
200-year-old ponderosa pine-tree or rock-specimens of gneiss and
schist of which the Front Range is largely composed. At one marker
a comparison could be made of the size and appearance of elk and
coyote droppings, and since there was a paragraph about them in the
guide booklet I assumed that these particular specimens had not been
deposited *in situ* by the animals themselves, but like glacial erratics
had been transported to that spot and dropped by some other
agency – in this case a human one. (I could visualise a park ranger in
his scout hat, periodically setting out in search of elk and coyote with
a shovel and two plastic bags in order to obtain fresh replacements
for the exhibits at Marker Seventeen.) Carefully designed to present
information about the vegetation, wild-life and geological history of
the locality within the compass of a forty-minute walk, these nature
trails were very popular with tourists of all kinds.

Although we had deliberately elected not to carry a trailer with
cooking stove and crockery (which friends had offered to lend us for
the tour), it was never difficult to obtain a meal for even the smallest
township seemed to possess a coffee-shop or restaurant which was
open from early morning to late evening, and we were impressed by
the cleanliness and service in American eating-places. We became
accustomed to the ritual procedure on entering a cafe: the waiter or
waitress would lay a paper place-mat on the table in front of each
person, with cutlery, paper napkin and a glass of ice-cold water.
These place-mats often contained interesting information about a
variety of topics, so we began to make a collection of them, one of
each kind, as the tour proceeded: route maps and details of local
topography and geology, incidents in the American Civil War,
pictures of veteran cars, crossword puzzles, the rush to the Rockies
in 1859 – they had the fascination which cigarette cards held for a
former generation of schoolboys, and the study of them helped to fill
in many an odd moment during our weeks of travel.

The Americans wisely provided parking space for cars off the
highway wherever a tourist attraction was present, whether it was a
scenic viewpoint, the site of an historical incident, or a feature of
geographical interest, and a brief description of the attraction was
given on a neat wooden board called a historical marker even though
the feature was not necessarily historical. A different kind of
roadside notice erected for the benefit of the traveller announced the
name of the city or township which was being entered, together with
a hint of civic pride in any additional details. We passed through
Castroville, a small township two kilometres out of Monterey on the
coast of California, which modestly claimed to be 'The artichoke
centre of the world', and I recall a handful of houses near Granite

Pass in the Bighorn Mountains of Wyoming, encountered on the return leg of our tour; a neatly painted sign introduced the hamlet with this information: 'Shell. Elevation 4,210 feet. Population 50.' The suburban areas of most large towns suffer from an uncontrolled rash of billboards and hoardings which are unsightly, garish and offensive to the conservationist who wishes to preserve the unspoilt appearance of the surroundings as far as possible, but in the deserted parts of the western states an occasional roadside notice directing the traveller to a motel or eating place is as welcoming as an oasis in the Sahara. The proprietors of a brand of shaving soap had erected a string of signs across the eremic expanses of Nevada and southern Utah which provided a welcome distraction when the landscape was monotonous and the afternoon heat soporific. These advertisements carried a rhyming couplet on four consecutive signs spaced at intervals of a few hundred yards, so that as we cruised along a lonely highway at sixty miles an hour we were able to read the complete message in a minute or two. Sometimes it contained advice about careful driving:

> Angels who guard you
> When you drive
> Usually retire
> At sixty-five.

This was a subtle reference to the speed-limit operating in that state. At other times it made a humorous reference, which might be historical or contemporary, to the advertiser's product:

> Henry the Eighth
> Sure had trouble
> Short term wives
> Long term stubble.

During our travels the fitted car radio proved to be a blessing, not merely for the news bulletins and weather forecasts giving warnings of impending storms but also to advise us of local time in the towns we were approaching, for although our coast-to-coast road map indicated the boundaries of the Standard Time Zones which we crossed every few days during the weeks we were heading west or east, I had not previously appreciated that townships and cities were free to adopt or reject Daylight Saving Time during the summer months. Hence the time could vary by an hour within one Time Zone; thus we discovered that Portland, Oregon, adopted DST and was therefore one hour ahead of Pacific Standard Time in July whereas the surrounding rural townships did not alter clocks and watches in the summer months. The difference of one hour was often crucial when we were planning to spend the night at a camping-ground, for the more attractive sites were often fully occupied by 5 p.m.

We spent four days in the oldest of America's national parks at Yellowstone where there is much to interest the visitor in its 8,800 km^2. The scenery is varied and impressive with its lakes, mountains and the canyon of the Yellowstone River, 360 m deep and 38 km long, exposing rock of every shade of yellow from pale lemon to brilliant orange due to the oxides of iron in the decomposed rhyolite. Thermal areas, with geysers, hot springs and mud volcanoes are scattered around the park, and the wild-life is omnipresent with the black bear as the tourists' greatest delight – and the park ranger's biggest headache. We watched an eruption of the most famous of the Yellowstone geysers, Old Faithful. It is a popular misconception, repeated in several books, that the geyser was given its name on account of the regularity of its eruptions – some books even state that it erupts on the hour, every hour. This is not true. The average interval between successive eruptions ranges from sixty-one to sixty-seven minutes, but it has been as long as ninety-five or as short as thirty-three minutes. Similarly, the length of play when it begins to erupt is not regular, but varies between two and five minutes. In 1938 a park ranger suddenly realised that there is a connection between the duration of Old Faithful's play and the length of the interval before the next eruption, so while we watched the geyser from a safe distance, a ranger with a microphone and stop-watch timed the length of the eruption and conveyed the details to the spectators and to a colleague in the nearby information centre, where a huge clock face was manually set to advise tourists of the time of the next eruption. A similar clock was visible in the nearby coffee shop, and as the time for the display approached many visitors hurriedly bolted the rest of their hamburgers and gulped down their coffee before dashing out as if to catch a departing train, but in reality to photograph the next eruption of Old Faithful.

We completed our seven-week tour by crossing Lake Michigan in a car-ferry steamer from Milwaukee to Muskegon, thereby avoiding the tedious drive through Chicago around the southern end of the lake. On the triangular journey between Michigan, California and British Columbia we had covered more than 13,200 km.

There is one sense which frequently makes a strong impression on the traveller yet is rarely mentioned in printed descriptions and cannot be conveyed directly by any picture, whether plain or coloured, moving or still. It is the sense of smell. To the voyager on

the high seas the next port of call has often been heralded, long
before the land comes into view, by a distinctive odour carried on the
breeze; it may be the smell of burning peat on the Falkland Islands in
the South Atlantic, the scent of orange groves on the Cape Verde
Islands farther north, or the sweetish rancid odour of drying
coconuts characteristic of islands in the tropics. Polynesians, who
without fuss travel thousands of kilometres in their frail canoes
between the far-flung groups of islands in the Pacific Ocean, often
take pigs on board during their longer journeys because pigs have a
highly developed sense of smell and they get excited as soon as they
can smell land even though it is still out of sight to the seamen.
Harold Gatty tells how he lost his bearings on a flight across the
eastern United States in a small aeroplane when the visibility was
very poor, but he was able to identify his position when he caught
a whiff of the glue factory which he knew was located on the
outskirts of the city of Philadelphia. Before the last war whenever
the London basin was blanketed by a thick fog, lightermen on the
Thames could tell which reach of the river they were in by the
distinctive smell. The odour of cinnamon and cloves indicated that
they were near the spice warehouses at Wapping Wall, while the
smell of malt signified Deptford Creek. I once made the journey
from Townsville to Cairns on a slow-moving, narrow-gauge train
comprising goods wagons and some passenger coaches, the latter
being crowded with Australian soldiers returning to duty in New
Guinea after a spell of home leave. The train made frequent lengthy
halts for no apparent reason and at about 9 p.m., when it shuddered
to yet another stop, I put my head out of the carriage window and at
once inhaled a heavy sweet smell which I have never forgotten; we
had halted alongside a sugar mill. A group of us walked up the track
to talk to the engine driver who reckoned that we would be
stationary for an hour or more, so upon receiving his assurance that
he would give us a warning blast on his whistle before he moved on,
we walked over to the mill and were courteously conducted on an
informal tour lasting forty minutes. With the passage of time I have
forgotten minor details of the successive stages whereby the cane was
crushed and the sugar extracted, but the powerfully strong sweet
smell of sugar in the warm evening air of Gordonvale remains vivid
in my memory.

Reference has already been made to the hot springs and geysers of
Yellowstone National Park. They look most attractive on a colour
transparency, but the picture fails to convey the stink of sulphuretted
hydrogen given off by these geysers, which causes many tourists to
grimace. Other vivid smells can be man-made. I recall walking along
the sea-front at Madras one evening after having dined with a college

principal. The route lay past a row of mud-hovels which can be seen in many parts of the city, cheek by jowl with impressive stone buildings, and although I had previously driven past groups of these slum shanties in a coach or taxi on several occasions my strongest recollection of them is related to the pungent odours emanating from these hovels which assailed my nostrils as I walked past them at midnight.

Children's noses are more sensitive to smells than are those of adults – they are closer to the ground, too, so that childhood memories which incorporate smells are often long remembered. Thus a middle-aged person, upon getting a whiff of decaying seaweed, will invariably recall a childhood visit to the seaside. There are distinctive smells associated with a bakery, a chocolate factory, a wood-pulp mill, a farmyard or a brewery, to give but a few examples. When a teacher evokes the atmosphere of a specific geographical environment, whether urban or rural, reference to the characteristic smells or scents of the neighbourhood can intensify the description of place. If the local town or countryside is sufficiently productive of scents and smells some children or groups of college students might be willing – and amused – to make an olfactory survey of their neighbourhood, plotting on a base map of suitable scale the source and strength of each distinctive odour. It would be necessary to devise a numerical pungency scale equivalent to a qualitative range extending from 'sickening' to 'odourless'. Once this had been done isolines could be drawn tentatively on the map, radiating from each source to indicate its sphere of influence. The stronger the smell, the closer together and more numerous would be the isolines (perhaps we could call them isoniffs or isopongs?) and of course it would be important to record the velocity and direction of the prevailing wind at the time of the survey, for a strong wind would distort the pattern of concentric circles into other shapes. Follow-up work in school or college might involve correlating the pungency scale with the grades of housing in the area. At least this exercise in common scents would bring home to the youthful surveyors the simple fact that within the broad belt of prevailing westerly winds the West End of a town or city is generally more attractive to live in than the East End.

In one of his Essays, Francis Bacon declared that in the younger sort, travel is a part of education, while in the elder, it is part of experience. Yet for many people, whatever their age, travel happily provides a bit of both.

REFERENCES

Francis Bacon, *The Essays or Counsels, Civil and Moral* (1625), ed. S. H. Reynolds (London, Oxford University Press, 1890), p. 125.
Peter Fleming, *Brazilian Adventure* (London, Odyssey Library, 1966), ch. 3.
Harold Gatty, *Nature Is Your Guide* (London, Collins, 1958), ch. 7.
Thor Heyerdahl, *The Kon-Tiki Expedition* (London, Allen & Unwin, 1950).
Robin Knox-Johnston, *A World of my Own* (London, Cassell, 1969).
Hugh Robert Mill, *The Record of the Royal Geographical Society, 1830–1930* (London, Royal Geographical Society, 1930), pp. 149–50.
J. A. Morris, 'Reality in geographical education', *Geography*, vol. 51, 1966, p. 91.
Tim Severin, *The Brendan Voyage* (London, Hutchinson, 1978).

Chapter 7

Picturesque Prose and Cursory Rhymes

The transmission of geographical data is generally accomplished by means of maps, graphs, diagrams, models, statistical tables or photographs, devices which supplement (or on occasion supplant) the basic text. The latter tends to be formal, solemn and prosaic, calculated to inform rather than entertain, for as befits the subject the language of geography is down-to-earth, lacking frills or refinements. Some years ago in a presidential address to the Institute of British Geographers H. C. Darby complained that professional geographers rarely write good descriptions of rural landscapes or urban scenes; they may give us details about the economy, history or geomorphology of an area, but they do not convey to us what a townscape or landscape really looks like. The geographer strives to be scientific in measuring and recording the elements which combine to give a distinctive appearance to a region, so that his approach is quantitative and unbiased, lacking any emotional involvement. On the other hand the expression of feeling is an art form, hence the novelist, painter or professional writer often proves to be more successful than the geographer in giving a colourful description of what it feels like to belong to a particular region. The contribution of literature has been the theme of a number of articles in different geographical journals wherein are examined, for example, topographical subdivisions of Wessex in the novels of Thomas Hardy, Scotland as it is portrayed in the romances of Sir Walter Scott, and Francis Brett Young's delineation of landscapes and life in the Black Country in his novels of the West Midlands. On the less exalted plane of geography in school it is equally important that the mundane facts and statistics of the textbook should be supplemented by more colourful detail in order to stimulate interest in the world around. It is true that few pupils nowadays are restricted to the use of a single all-purpose textbook for their information since it has become increasingly common for a number of different supplementary books or booklets, each concerned with one topic or one region, to be on the reference shelves in the geography room.

Moreover, instead of trying to study a large natural region, the modern trend is to select a sample farm, factory, valley or village for more detailed study as a typical specimen of the human activity common to a much wider area. There are now several excellent books of sample studies available to teachers for class use, with numerous farm-plans, a calendar of seasonal activities, photographs of the farmer and his family, and a hint of how he spends his leisure-time. Yet even these detailed accounts are severely practical in presentation. They describe the labourer's daily routine from dawn until midnight but they rarely reveal his feelings, his hopes and fears, or what he really thinks of his employer. To look at life from the worker's viewpoint and to view the region from within instead of looking at it objectively from the outside, novels can be more expressive than the geography textbook and for this reason every teacher should make a collection of well-written passages of prose, extracted from novels, for transmission to pupils or students. A few examples will suffice for many. The thoughts of the farming communities in Oklahoma during the prolonged drought of the 1930s as they resignedly watched the wind whip off the topsoil and wither away their grain crops is vividly told in *The Grapes of Wrath* by John Steinbeck. The bewilderment of the Bantu elder as he leaves the tribe to make his first visit to the brash, bustling city of Johannesburg in search of his daughter, symbolic of the clash of cultures in South Africa which was accentuated by the vigorous exploitation of its mineral resources, is conveyed beautifully in writing of stark simplicity in the pages of Alan Paton's novel *Cry the Beloved Country*. Finally, amid less exotic surroundings, the attitude towards his work of a factory-hand in the machine-shop in the English midlands who is engaged on a boring repetitive task day after day, is cleverly put into print in Alan Sillitoe's novel *Saturday Night and Sunday Morning*. Nevertheless, novels are not the only literary form which can convey geographical detail in a more vivid manner than the average textbook. Travel books, biographies, editorials in newspapers, articles in popular magazines, all can be drawn upon for supplementary matter. Grace King has compiled a delightful anthology of more than 300 prose passages to illustrate the hardships and rewards experienced by human beings acting out their lives against diverse landscapes; it is entitled *Conflict and Harmony: A Source-Book of Man in his Environment*. This book invites comparison with a similar anthology which was published nearly twenty years previously by the same firm: this was *Splendour of Earth*, compiled by Marion Anderson.

Some textbooks, it has to be admitted, are more attractively written than others, but in general the limitations of space and the authors' desire to include as many essentials as possible result in books which are read as a duty rather than as a pleasure. The nineteenth-century French geographer Elisée Reclus wrote many volumes in a literary style which was widely praised, but there have been few to match him in the English language. American geographers have been more inclined than their colleagues in Britain to write textbooks in a lively, almost racy style, and some older teachers may recall the pleasure they experienced during their own schooldays of dipping into the first edition of J. Russell Smith's *North America*. Replete with lively anecdotes this bulky college text held the reader's attention from the opening lines of the first chapter:

'Hell is hot. Did you ever wonder why? But not all Hells are hot ... '

This dramatic opening was replaced by a more subdued introduction in later editions of this book, perhaps in order to bring it into line with the sober presentation of standard texts?

When school geographies were unashamedly dull and their contents resembled a cross between a gazetteer and an encyclopaedia, some attempt to assist the assimilation of data was made by resorting to verse-form, presumably on the principle that boring details could be committed to memory more readily if they were rendered in rhyme. In the year of the British naval victory at Trafalgar *The Geographical Guide* was published in London. Compiled by J. Bisset and subtitled *A Poetical Nautical Trip round the Island of Great Britain*, it neatly enumerated the ins and outs of the coastline in verse of this calibre:

> Round England and Scotland prepare for a trip,
> And whilst British Tars are unmooring the ship,
> We'll over a map of the isles take a glance,
> Then start from Land's End and sail round by Penzance.
> Mount's Bay having crossed, by the Lizard then steer
> Your course to North-East and by North quickly veer.

A similar prescription was used to describe the economic importance of places, whether coastal or inland; *Geography in Verse* was published in London in 1845, and after reading a specimen stanza one can perhaps appreciate why the author preferred to remain anonymous:

> Next Yorkshire this county of large towns is full,
> Here's the capital, York, then there's Beverley, Hull,
> Leeds, Bradford and Halifax, Huddersfield too
> All famous for cloth as perhaps you well know,
> While southward lies Sheffield where trade briskly thrives
> In goods silver-plated, forks, razors and knives.

A more sophisticated conception of the subject could hardly be purveyed by doggerel of this nature, however, and as soon as geography had acquired a respectable position in the curriculum it became undeniably prosaic. There were exceptions, of course. William Wordsworth wrote sensitively about the English Lake District in many of his poems, while more than a century later the regional variety of scenery in England was outlined in verse by Francis Brett Young in his epic poem *The Island*. Nevertheless it would probably be conceded that nowadays any geography which is rendered in verse tends to be light-hearted in tone, superficial in content and illustrative rather than fundamental, its function being to inject a little levity into more ponderous matters. Consider, for example, the following verse, taken from G. K. Chesterton's *Song of Education*:

> Our principal exports, all labelled and packed,
> At the ends of the earth are delivered intact:
> Our soap or our salmon can travel in tins
> Between the two poles and as like as two pins;
> So that Lancashire merchants whenever they like
> Can water the beer of a man in Klondyke
> Or poison the meat of a man in Bombay
> And that is the meaning of Empire Day.

One sector of geographical studies which seems to attract more verse than others is the field of climate and meteorology. There is an old saying which asserts with some truth that 'Providence gave the Englishman his weather in order to make him articulate in the presence of strangers', and it is remarkable how this topic, which provokes a greater volume of superficial conversation among the general public than does any other branch of geography, should become so dull and statistical when it is studied in depth. The eminent scientist and geographer S. W. Wooldridge once declared that 'before the age of generalisation is attained few things are more sterile than the generalisations of climatology' and it would seem that the *effects* of climate and weather are more interesting than their *causes* to the man-in-the-street, who is less concerned with the physics of a thunderstorm than with the possibility that it might ruin his game of cricket on Saturday afternoon. Is it because the explanation of climate and weather to the uninitiated is so much a boring business of mean monthly averages and concepts of changing atmosphere pressure that writers deliberately choose to enliven their scientific texts with scattered quotations of verse to aid the mental digestion? Every chapter of Gordon Manley's book on the climate of the British Isles opens with a few lines from the works of Milton, Shakespeare, Shelley, Wordsworth and other poets, while a few quotations of verse creep into the text too. C. R. Benstead's discourse on meteorology follows the same pattern to an even greater degree, with poetic extracts appearing in each chapter as frequently as showers in April. Weather forecasting and verse have long been associated, of course, everyone is familiar with certain rhyming couplets about the weather, so ancient that they have acquired the force of lore:

> Red sky at night
> Is the shepherd's delight.
> Red sky in the morning
> Is the shepherd's warning.

> The north wind doth blow
> And we shall have snow.

> Rain before seven,
> Fine before eleven.

> When ditch and pond offend the nose,
> Then look for rain and stormy blows.

In mediaeval times, when the church exercised a more powerful influence upon the lives of ordinary men and women than it does today, and holidays were associated with holy days, it was common practice to forecast weather from the meteorological conditions prevailing on a particular saint's day. St Swithin was not the only holy man to be linked with damp conditions, for it was said of St Vitus, whose day falls on 15 June:

> If St Vitus' Day be rainy weather
> It will rain for thirty days together.

It is possible to string together enough proverbs of this kind to prophesy that if it rains on a particular saint's day it will continue to be wet every day for eternity. This was probably the reason why in the reign of Henry VIII a proclamation was made against almanacks which printed belief in the saints ruling the weather. One of the best known of the wet-weather saints is Swithin, but a study of scientific observations made in south-eastern England over a sixty-three-year period has revealed that if it rains on 15 July it will be followed on average by no more than seventeen wet days out of the next forty. This accords with the experience of many parts of lowland Britain where on average almost every alternate day in the year is a rain day. A few of these old adages have an element of scientific truth in them, but the majority are pure superstition and hearsay, possibly amusing but certainly unreliable. During the present century the frontiers of knowledge concerning atmospheric conditions have been extended by meteorology rather than by paroemiology; it was accordingly a gracious gesture by the Royal Meteorological Society in 1950, as part of their centenary celebrations, to publish a revised edition of the delightful collection of sayings about the weather which had been gathered by Richard Inwards towards the end of the nineteenth century.

A. P. Herbert visualised meteorologists at work in this manner:

> In some high mansion, I suppose,
> The weather-men confront the stars,
> Giving 'the glass' tremendous blows
> And drinking deep at isobars.

Nevertheless, in spite of all their scientific apparatus and technical vocabulary the forecasters sometimes find that their predictions, like the depressions to which they are so often related, go astray ...

> The time has come, the met-man said,
> To show how wise we are;
> To play with cold occluded fronts,
> And kink the isobar;
> And tell how we know why the rain
> At stroke of two will clear.
> – I doubt it, said the cricketer
> And stowed away his gear.
> (Quoted in C. R. Benstead, *The Weather Eye*)

The absence of a regular annual dry season and the uncertainty of the weather at all times are two characteristic features of the climate of Britain (the prolonged summer drought of 1976 was exceptional). These features never fail to impress the overseas visitor to this island who marvels at the equable distribution over the whole year of the very modest annual average rainfall experienced in south-eastern England. This fact must have been uppermost in the mind of the cynic who wrote:

> Dirty days hath September,
> April, June and November;
> From January up till May
> The rain it raineth every day.
> All the rest have thirty-one
> Without a blessed gleam of sun;
> And if any of them had two-and-thirty
> They'd be just as wet and twice as dirty.

It's funny that he *should be out in front just as we move on to the Bunter Sandstone*

One verse form of five lines which at first sight appears to be geographical is the limerick, with a distinctive rhyme pattern and a function designed to amuse rather than instruct. Its origin is often attributed to Edward Lear although as Cyril Bibby has demonstrated in his book *The Art of the Limerick* humorous verse in limerick form existed long before Lear popularised this type of poem in his *Book of Nonsense*, published in the middle of the nineteenth century. The name may have been derived from a custom at parties in Ireland whereby individuals took turns to compose an impromptu nonsense verse to which the entire company chanted a chorus containing the words 'Will you come up to Limerick?'. But this derivation lacks positive proof and Bibby offers alternative explanations which are

just as plausible. The first line of a limerick commonly ends in a
place-name which locates the central character of the verse. This
might be a young man from Devizes whose ears were of different
sizes, or an old man of Calcutta who coated his tonsils with butter or
an epicure dining at Crewe who found quite a large mouse in his
stew . . . However, since the bulk of the verse is concerned more with
the eccentricities of an individual than with peculiarities of place, a
passing reference to a locality scarcely justifies considering a limerick
as geographical although Bibby mentions in his book a pamphlet by
an unknown author which was published in London in 1913 under
the title *Geography without Groans: A Few Words on the Use of
Limericks in County Council Schools*. However, very few limericks
convey reliable geographical data about the place mentioned.
Consider, for example, the following specimen which appeared as
long ago as 1822 in a book probably compiled by Richard Scrafton
Sharpe under the title of *Adventures and Anecdotes of Fifteen
Gentlemen*:

> There was a sick man of Tobago
> Lived long on rice-gruel and sago
> But at last to his bliss
> The physician said this –
> 'To a roast leg of mutton you may go'.

This anecdote in rhyme adds little to our geographical knowledge of
this West Indian island.

Since Edward Lear's time the limerick has become more
sophisticated and it now offers a vehicle for all manner of witticisms
and word-play, some of which are scarcely fit to be printed.
Nevertheless, there are a few which have their uses in the geography
lesson, one of them giving a guide to the pronunciation of certain
places which do not sound the way one would expect from their
spelling. In the adult version of this type of limerick the terminal
words of the second and fifth lines are not spelled correctly but
imitate the devious spelling of the place-name at the end of the first
line, with which they rhyme. I have composed the following as an
example of the type:

> There was an old lady in Drogheda
> Who spent hours learning how to embrogheda
> But her failure with stitches
> Made her bad-tempered, which is
> Why everyone tried to avogheda.

If the reader does not already know the pronunciation of the place

mentioned in the first line it requires some alertness of mind and eye
to decipher the word in line two which gives a clue to its
pronunciation. If examples of this kind of limerick are given to
pupils of only moderate ability it might be desirable to rewrite them
with the word at the end of line two spelled correctly i.e. as
'embroider' in the example quoted. However, if it is felt that such
treatment destroys the charm of this type of limerick the
convolutions of spelling should be retained and offered only to
pupils who are bright enough to appreciate word-play. There are
limericks in this category concerning eccentrics from Alnwick,
Beaulieu, and Towcester to provide amusing hints on correct
pronunciation for the youngster in English schools, while quite a
number of adults in Britain can learn how to pronounce some
American places by reading limericks about persons in Butte, Des
Moines and Duquesne. In addition to the specimens quoted by Cyril
Bibby in his book, others can be found in *The Pan Book of
Limericks* edited by Louis Untermeyer and in the collection
assembled in America by Bennett Cerf entitled *Out on a Limerick*.

Another type of limerick which has its uses for the student of
geography employs an abbreviated form of the terminal word in the
first line and then coins a similar abbreviation for the rhyming words
at the end of lines two and five. Americans commonly print a
shortened version for most of the states in the Union; some of these,
for example, Calif., Colo., Tenn. or Mass., can be identified with
ease because they comprise the first few letters of the full word,
whereas others such as Ga, Md, Mo, La, Pa or Va require some
elucidation by the geography pupil in Britain. The following
limerick, which I have invented as an illustration, contains the
abbreviated form of two of the United States of America. If these
are read aloud in full they will give a clue to the rhyming words
which have been disguised by equivalent abbreviations:

> A geography student in Me
> Sought relief from the cold winds and re.
> So he flew south to Fla
> Where the climate is ta
> Though the chief crop is not sugar-ce.

There are several examples of this type of limerick in Bennett
Cerf's little book which will test the ability of the reader to interpret
American state abbreviations. In view of the continued popularity of
limerick competitions in weekly magazines and newspapers, both for
children and adults, some teachers may like to encourage their
brighter pupils to compile specimens similar to the two which I have

quoted above. If that proves too difficult a task for immature minds, a less exacting assignment would be to provide the class with the first four lines of a limerick and then invite them to supply a suitable last line. Just as the multiple-choice tests which are used in school can be derived from one of the published collections of tests or can be devised by the teacher, so the first four lines of a limerick can be obtained from one of the publications already named, or can be 'home-made'.

Rhymes which have been set to music may possess a more popular appeal than ordinary verse and moreover they can sometimes be remembered better. Certain songs make reference to particular places although few go as far as to convey useful geographical information. Light ballads have been composed about the banks of Loch Lomond, the mountains of Mourne and the lakes of Killarney, suggesting that the Celtic fringe of Highland Britain is a favoured locale for writers of romantic songs, but apart from London and Glasgow scarcely any British cities have become the subject of songs sung around the piano or camp-fire or on the stage, and in spite of its popularity as a community and marching song through two world wars, Tipperary remains for the masses an enigmatic destination as remote and mysterious as Lhasa.

American composers appear to have discovered more romantic associations in the place-names of their native land, both rural and urban, than have their British counterparts, so that many people in Britain probably think of American states and cities, not in terms of the details taught during formal geography lessons in their schooldays (most of which they have probably forgotten), but by virtue of phrases in popular songs heard on radio or television or in cinema, theatre or club. In this way they remember that Broadway, 42nd Street and Central Park are in the heart of New York, that State Street is that great street in Chicago, San Francisco is where the little cable-cars climb halfway to the stars, and that nothing could be finer than to be in Carolina in the morning – unless it is to be west of the Mississippi in Oklahoma when the corn is as high as an elephant's eye. Although the geographical detail in them may be trivial, these popular songs undoubtedly help to create images of places which many ordinary people have never visited. Moreover, they often make a more lasting impression on a young person than details taught formally in school, so that a few lines or bars of an old song will recall for an elderly man or woman some personal incident with which that song was associated when it was first heard in their youthful days, many years before.

Although many songs contain a slender reference to places, it is extremely rare to find one which has a geographical theme running through it. An outstanding example of this type is the amusing ballad *Mad Dogs and Englishmen* which was written and composed by Noel Coward in 1932. Coward shared with W. S. Gilbert the gift of writing humorous verse full of wit and charm, with the words tumbling forth in such profusion that it is difficult to catch and savour fully every phrase at a single hearing. This satirical treatment of the behaviour of Englishmen in tropical climates, contrasted with that of the indigenous peoples, is quoted in full in *A Century of Humorous Verse 1850–1950*, edited by R. L. Green. It would provide relief from more serious studies if a recording of this song were to be played to a geography class, inviting the listeners to judge the accuracy of Noel Coward's perception of tropical regions by making a list of the groups of men or beasts named in the song which are not truly amphiscian.

In recent years there has been a revival of interest in country music and folk songs which contain a wealth of detail about the labouring classes. Ballads about the teams of men who built railways, navvies engaged in canal construction, impoverished hill-farmers in the backwoods of Kentucky, coal miners in Durham or cutlery grinders in Sheffield may teach a child more than he gains from a textbook simply because of the colourful and melodious way in which the material is presented. Radio and television programmes for schools are increasingly using this medium to supplement the more orthodox and prosaic way of conveying information about the life and livelihood of ordinary folk in different lands.

Finally, a word of caution. The serious geographer views with suspicion any rendering of material in verse or song because the words have to be chosen to fit the metre and poetic licence may tempt the composer into perpetrating geographical inaccuracies. One example will illustrate this point. Arnold Weissberger in his album of portraits entitled *Famous Faces* tells how one year he was influenced by Vernon Duke's song *April in Paris* to pay a visit to the French capital in that month. It turned out to be miserably cold and wet with rain every day of his visit. Later that summer he met the writer of the song who asked him about his recent travels. When Weissberger told him that he had been to Paris in April, Duke asked 'Why did you do that? The weather is terrible at that time of the year.' Weissberger exclaimed in astonishment 'But Vernon, I went because of your song!' To which the composer replied, 'Well, I really meant to write May, but the rhythm required two syllables.'

REFERENCES

M. S. Anderson, *Splendour of Earth. An Anthology of Travel* (London, George Philip, 1954).

C. R. Benstead, *The Weather Eye* (London, Robert Hale, 1940).

C. Bibby, *The Art of the Limerick* (London, The Research Publishing Co, 1978).

J. Bisset, *Geographical Guide: A Poetical, Nautical Trip round the Island of Great Britain* (London, J. Harris, 1805).

Bennett Cerf, *Out on a Limerick* (New York, Pocket Books, 1962).

G. K. Chesterton, 'Songs of Education II. Geography', in *The Collected Poems of G. K. Chesterton* (London, Methuen, 1942).

Noel Coward, 'Mad dogs and Englishmen', in R. L. Green (ed.), *A Century of Humorous Verse, 1850–1950* (London, Dent, 1959) pp. 251–3.

H. C. Darby, 'The problem of geographical description', *Transactions of the Institute of British Geographers*, 1962, pp. 1–14.

R. Inwards, *Weather Lore*, ed. and rev. E. L. Hawke (London, Rider & Co. for the Royal Meteorological Society, 1950).

Grace E. King (ed.), *Conflict and Harmony: A Source-Book of Man in his Environment* (London, George Philip, 1972)

Gordon Manley, *Climate and the British Scene* (London, Collins, 1952).

R. S. Sharpe, *Adventures and Anecdotes of Fifteen Gentlemen* (London, John Marshall, 1822).

Louis Untermeyer (ed.), *The Pan Book of Limericks* (London, Pan, 1963).

L. Arnold Weissberger, *Famous Faces: A Photograph Album of Personal Reminiscences* (New York, Abrams, n.d.) p. 242.

S. W. Wooldridge, 'On taking the 'ge-' out of geography', *Geography*, vol. 34, 1949, pp. 9–18.

Francis Brett Young, 'Many-coloured isle', in *The Island* (London, Heinemann, 1944), pp. 378–86.

Chapter 8

A Little Judicious Levity

Although each of the preceding chapters can be regarded as a
separate essay on a selected geographical topic, they are tenuously
linked by a number of concepts, overt or implicit, which recur at
irregular intervals throughout these pages. It would accordingly seem
appropriate at this point to identify these concepts and consider them
in a little more detail, since they represent the foundations upon
which the book has been written.

(1) *The teaching of geography at the present time is influenced, more
than we may realise, by reaction against the theories and practice of
our predecessors.*
  The scope and content of geography in school and the methods
employed to teach it have evolved during the last two hundred years
or so, although the rate of change has not been constant.
Development has been akin to the mountain-building of geological
history whereby episodes of vigorous upheaval have been separated
by long intervals of comparative stability. The first seventy years of
the last century formed one of the quiescent periods as a prelude to
the Hercynian activity which was initiated by the rumblings of the
Royal Geographical Society and sustained by the exertions of
Halford Mackinder and A. J. Herbertson at Oxford around the turn
of the century. Two world wars and their aftermaths coincided with
a phase of consolidation and relative stability before the Alpine
storm of intense reappraisal and innovation broke during the 1960s
and 1970s, an orogeny whose thrusts and reverberations have not yet
subsided.
  In 1800 geography was widely taught in Britain through the use of
globes. Raggedly clad pupils in charity schools and elegant daughters
of prosperous gentlemen attending private academies were all taught
the position of towns on the globe in terms of latitude and longitude,
details which then had to be committed to the memory for
subsequent recital, parrot-fashion. It was a practice reinforced by the
textbooks of the time. *The Use of the Globes and the Rudiments of
Geography*, originally written by Daniel Fenning, was corrected and
improved by Joseph Moon for the seventh edition, published in
1798. It contained eighty pages of 'problems', that is, exercises on

the identification of places and physical features by the use of globes. The revulsion of later generations of teachers against this narrow concept of geography may well explain in large measure the neglect of the globe as a teaching aid during the present century.

In the course of time wall-maps performed a similar function to the globes of an earlier generation. The greater detail which could be conveyed on a map of the British Isles gave rise to a form of teaching which required children to identify the many headlands and inlets around the coast in addition to the chief towns and rivers. This concept of rote-learning now stands condemned on at least two counts: it excluded more stimulating ways of studying geographical phenomena, and it failed to distinguish between important and unimportant details. 'Capes and bays' geography did not select the significant from the mass of minor facts so that it placed an unnecessary burden on the learner's memory; as a technique it was comparable to the method of requiring children to learn by heart all the entries on a page of the dictionary, instead of concentrating attention on the more common words. Reaction against excessive and unselective memory-work has persisted to this day and probably accounts for the reluctance of many teachers to enforce the learning of even a modicum of the most important geographical locations which are encountered during formal lessons.

Throughout much of the nineteenth century the subject-matter of geography was separated into two distinct compartments. On the one hand there was general geography, a confusing gallimaufry of items about people, places and products. By contrast, physical geography shared in the greater prestige which was accorded geology in academic circles. When Mackinder was appointed Reader in geography at Oxford University in 1887 he was determined to bring together the sundered halves of the subject and to enhance the status of human geography. He subsequently summarised the situation in these words:

'In this country the geologists had captured Physical Geography and had laid it out as a garden for themselves, while the remnant known as "General Geography" was a no-man's land encumbered with weeds and dry bones. Before British Geography could come into its own again it was necessary to re-annex the garden and to clear and cultivate the waste.'

Mackinder sought to unite the human and physical elements within a framework of regional studies and in this conception of the scope and method of the subject he was ably assisted by A. J. Herbertson whose subdivision of the land-masses into Major Natural Regions offered teachers a means of simplifying the mass of detail about the world before presenting it to children. The reaction against the dominating role formerly played by physical geography persisted well into the present century and it was expressed with some force at a conference of the Geographical Association in 1913. Speaking in the discussion which followed an address by C. B. Fawcett on the teaching of landforms, James Fairgrieve declared:

'I feel myself, from experience, that we have not the time to teach it [physical geography] as an independent subject ... It is regional treatment along definite lines that must form the framework of our geographical teaching in our syllabuses, but we must manage to work in this Physical Geography incidentally.'

This unequivocal viewpoint was subsequently conveyed to hundreds of teachers during the interwar years, for until his retirement in 1935 Fairgrieve was lecturer in geography method at the London Day Training College which later became the Institute of Education in the University of London. His opinions were transmitted to many more through his articles and textbooks, but above all in his manual of method entitled *Geography in School*, first published in 1926, which for thirty years was unrivalled as a guide to teachers.

By the middle of this century there were signs of a reaction against the subordinate position of physical geography in the secondary school syllabus. S. W. Wooldridge protested at the exclusion of geomorphology from the hybrid subject which was appearing in some schools after the war as social studies, while teachers in conference voiced criticisms of the dominant regional pattern of grammar school geography. However, opposition to the status quo was sporadic and unorganised until residential courses for 'teachers of pre-university geography' (a significant designation!) were held at Madingley Hall near Cambridge in the early 1960s. The first fruit of these gatherings was the publication of a collection of essays edited by Richard Chorley and Peter Haggett under the title of *Frontiers in Geographical Teaching*, which was severely critical of the unscientific and regionally organised geography currently being taught in schools. This book appeared in 1965, precisely half a century after the death of Herbertson, and it signalled a vigorous reassessment of the concepts underlying the scope of geography in school. Recommendations for the use of quantitative methods, theoretical models, stochastic processes, simulations and network analyses poured from a stream of books and articles written by Chorley and Haggett and their followers. The rate at which these ideas were

implemented in schools was understandably slower than the speed
with which they were printed, for dramatic changes in secondary
education can rarely be accomplished without certain favourable
conditions; these include time for teachers to absorb the new ideas
before they are capable of transmitting them, the production of
textbooks incorporating the new techniques, and appropriate
revision of the syllabuses prepared by the major examination boards
to set the seal of approval on the emerging concepts of study. Major
changes of this kind cannot be effected overnight. An *Education
Survey* published by the Department of Education and Science in
1974 reported an investigation conducted by Her Majesty's
Inspectors into a sample of secondary schools in England and Wales
two years earlier. It revealed that games and simulations had been
adopted in 35 per cent of the schools, quantitative methods in 29 per
cent, theoretical models in 24 and networks in 11 per cent. Only one-
fifth of the schools surveyed were employing a combination of more
than one of these four techniques.

(2) *Teaching is not solely concerned with fundamental facts and
concepts; there is a time and place for trivia.*

Children have an uncanny flair for remembering minor details
while forgetting the important items. I once had occasion to use a
school textbook on South America written by E. V. Lane in a series
published by Harrap. It was packed with geographical facts to
provide me with copious notes and material for several essays. Yet
down the years the only item in that book which I can now recall is
the statement that Georgetown probably had the finest cricket
ground in the tropics. In those days it was unusual to find references
to sport in a staid textbook so I imagine that I remembered this item
because it stood out from the mass of humdrum geographical details
concerning relief, climate and commerce. (In my youth most regional
texts on America mentioned the importance of the pitch in Trinidad
but that was not the kind on which cricket was played!) Every
generation of youngsters tends to remember details because of the
circumstances in which they were presented at the time, and often it
is a trivial classroom joke or piece of childish word-play which helps
to fix an item in the memory. Before the Second World War it was
commonplace to think of the Germans and Russians as being Poles
apart, while a reference to Dantzig in the Polish Corridor conjured
up a youthful vision of waltzing couples whirling around in evening
dress. As for the nascent Baltic port of Gdynia, it was always
remembered by one group of young geographers because it was
formally brought to their notice in a lesson soon after Bing Crosby
had made a recording of a popular new song entitled 'A Little White

Gardenia'. Coincidence and association play an important part in aiding the memory.

A geography syllabus which has been prepared with care will ensure that at the appropriate stage in the course children will be taught the basic skills of map-making, map-interpretation, field-sketching and the analysis of climatic and economic statistics. They will also be introduced to fundamental concepts relating to geomorphology, meteorology, industrial location, urban settlement and population distribution. Topics which develop these themes will tend to occupy a major part of every lesson but whether the emphasis is laid on understanding facts or concepts the going will be heavy if the entire time is taken up with these serious matters. An occasional digression onto a minor, almost inconsequential item is not only desirable, but it may well reinforce the main theme. How often have adults welcomed a light anecdote or touch of word-play in an otherwise serious sermon or public address? The wise teacher will build up a personal collection of trivia from all available sources – conferences, after-dinner speeches, novels, newspaper columns and letters from friends or relatives, in addition to the standard textbooks and journals – so that he can introduce them, whenever appropriate, as light interludes between more weighty matters. A few of these minor items are given by way of illustration.

The diversification of farming in the cotton belt of the United States which followed upon the ravages of the cotton boll-weevil prompted the inhabitants of the township of Enterprise in southern Alabama to erect a public monument to the weevil in 1919, for it was the incursions of this pest which had led to a drastic change of economy. The farmers of Enterprise were no longer solely dependent upon the cotton crop, for they had turned to the production of peanuts and the rearing of cattle and pigs, diverse activities which had brought them unexpected prosperity.

The fondness of the Russians for conveying statistics in terms of percentages instead of absolute numbers reached absurd lengths in the annual report for a remote outpost in Siberia which included a statement that during the preceding year 2 per cent of the men had married 50 per cent of the women. This would seem to imply an outbreak of polygamy until it is realised that the pioneer settlement consisted of fifty men and two women, and one of the men had married one of the women to produce this statistical item!

The millions of tons of silt carried annually along in suspension by the Colorado River in the western USA led one American observer to describe the river in somewhat exaggerated terms as 'too thick to drink, yet too thin to plough'.

One of the photographs in the book on soil erosion by Jacks and Whyte shows a gully in Basutoland (Lesotho) which had been started unintentionally by villagers taking a short cut across a field. The constant passage of many pairs of bare feet along the path destroyed the vegetation on it, and torrential rains washed away the exposed soil to form a deep cleft across the field. The picture showed a Bantu holding a pole three metres in length which nevertheless was not long enough to reach the bottom of the donga.

The absence of trees and fences and the abundance of cattle in the Argentine pampas before the invention of refrigeration are illustrated in the story of the gaucho who killed a steer merely to enable him to hitch his horse to the horns of the fallen beast while he rested from work to take his mid-day siesta.

The arid climate of Arizona was neatly conveyed in the photograph of a motel in Yuma which carried a notice running the entire length of the verandah bearing these words: 'Free board every day the sun doesn't shine'.

Some trivia are brief enough to be epigrammatic, such as the apt description of Edinburgh as the 'East Windy, West Endy city'.

Minor geographical details of this sort are plentiful enough to fill an entire book, but perhaps sufficient examples have been given here and throughout the preceding chapters to demonstrate their value as supplementary illustrations of major themes.

(3) *There are important differences in the attitude of children to the geography which is taught in school and to that which is learnt informally elsewhere.*

From the moment that geography became an established subject in the school curriculum it acquired a structure and a technical language of its own which is unfamiliar to the layman. With the passage of time, as more thought is given to the philosophy of the discipline, it develops a theoretical component which diverges more and more from the popular conception of the subject; it was this distinctive corpus of knowledge and the peculiar technique of formal study of history and geography in school which Sellar and Yeatman satirised so delightfully in their books *1066 and All That* and *And Now All This*. Moreover, in the later stages of study in the secondary school, geography tends to be taught along the lines laid down by the syllabus of the examining board which conducts external Certificate examinations. For this reason it is usually more difficult to vary the teaching of the subject in the upper school where examinations exert pressure on the teacher to conform to the prescribed syllabus.

On the other hand the geography which is absorbed by the child informally outside the school is a piecemeal, disordered collection of items, lacking a coherent structure or sequence of study. Comics, works of fiction, radio, television and the cinema, glossy magazines, picture postcards, foreign stamps, cigarette cards, cut-out models printed on cartons of breakfast foods, all supply scraps of information, with varying degrees of accuracy, offered to the individual. In spite of the fact that they lack logical order or arrangement, these items which have been acquired haphazardly tend to be remembered more readily simply because they have been accepted voluntarily by the individual and not forced upon him by a teacher. A parent once bought his son a few hundred assorted foreign stamps and an album of the kind which arranges the stamp-issuing countries alphabetically from Abyssinia to Zanzibar, hoping that by this means the lad would pick up information about the various parts of the world in an easy informal manner. After a few weeks the father sought to test his son's progress by asking him where was Colombia, and quick as a flash came the answer – 'between China and Cuba'! Another parent took his daughter to London when she was about 9 years old to show her the historic sights. She remained unimpressed by the Houses of Parliament, Tower of London and St Paul's Cathedral, which failed to arouse any enthusiasm for her national heritage, until she was given a booklet entitled *I-Spy London*, purchased from a newsagent's shop. The idea of scoring points for discovering specific features about buildings and monuments provided just the right stimulus to arouse her interest, and for the rest of the stay in London she trailed her parents to and fro in an excited attempt to run up a respectable score by discovering, for instance, the item missing from Boadicea's chariot at the northern end of Westminster Bridge, or the creatures carved around the base of Cleopatra's Needle on the Embankment.

Sometimes the geography teacher can with profit diverge from the carefully designed programme of lessons in order to insert an 'eccentric' lesson which relates to a topical news incident or which is strongly requested by the class. J. T. White tells how he discarded a carefully prepared lesson on cocoa farms in Nigeria, part of a series of studies on tropical Africa, in order to satisfy the urgent request of his 'academically-ungifted' (*sic*) pupils who clamoured for a lesson on China. It appeared that on the previous evening many of the class had been to see a Chinese juggler performing in the back streets of London, a spectacle which had apparently aroused in them a fierce interest in the inhabitants of China. (The teacher subsequently discovered that the juggler was not Chinese but Japanese!) The extent to which an impromptu lesson requested by the class can be delivered successfully will depend largely upon the knowledge, experience and panache of the teacher. Sometimes, however, the tables can be turned and the teacher may surprise the class by switching attention away from the expected lesson to deal instead with the background to an item which has suddenly become prominent in the news, whether it be a violent local storm, mass murders in Manhattan or an earthquake in Iran.

Of course, not all formal geography taught in school is necessarily dull or boring, and not all geography encountered informally by the child outside school turns out to be entertaining. Nevertheless, there is usually a marked contrast in the attitude of the pupil towards that which is thrust upon him and that which he acquires incidentally or voluntarily. It is helpful if the teacher can utilise the enthusiasm which is generated by the informal acquisition of knowledge and harness it to the geography taught in school. Moreover, if the teacher makes a practice of inviting his pupils to contribute geographical items which they have picked up outside the classroom to supplement the information which he presents to them in formal lessons, he will gain a valuable insight into the structures of knowledge governing learning experience as distinct from teaching experience. The use of trivial details at judicious intervals, a certain resilience in the programme of lessons to permit the introduction of the occasional surprise item, and a few touches of humour to convey the teacher's enjoyment of the situation, can all contribute to this end.

(4) *The teacher's personal enjoyment of geography should be a powerful means of encouraging pupils to develop an interest in the subject.*

For obvious reasons specialists tend to derive more pleasure from teaching their chosen subject than any other. Their original decision to specialise in that field was probably made because they were attracted to it in the first place, while the subsequent study of it in depth gave them increased confidence as their knowledge and understanding developed. At the tertiary stage of education this attraction takes the form of reading widely, participating in seminars, field excursions and researching for a long essay or dissertation. Some re-evaluation takes place when the student turns teacher and discovers that much of the detail studied at the college or undergraduate level is not used in school, while the frequent repetition of elementary facts and processes to junior classes may prove a little monotonous. There are two ways of preventing teaching from becoming a bore. One is to follow some aspect of geography to a more advanced level than is required for teaching in school, whether in the shape of study for a higher degree, the preparation of an article for a learned journal, or attendance at courses and conferences. The alternative is to become interested in the technique of teaching the subject, as distinct from the advanced study of the subject itself; for example, instead of reading in depth about the history of cartography one could devise classroom tests similar to those described in the second chapter, to estimate the proportion of children in any particular age-group who appreciate the deficiencies of the world maps which appear in the standard school atlas.

Unfortunately for many enthusiastic teachers, the zeal with which they approach their work is accompanied by such a seriousness of intent that they run the risk of cutting themselves off from normal communication with their pupils instead of transmitting to them their enjoyment of the subject. Foremost among the many great qualities of Dr Skinner, headmaster of Roughborough Grammar School, was his childlike earnestness – 'an earnestness which might be perceived by the solemnity with which he spoke even about trifles'. This character in Samuel Butler's novel *The Way of All Flesh* believed in the importance of being earnest, but there is a danger in displaying this quality to excess. The teacher who is so absorbed in his subject that he becomes oblivious to the impact of his words upon his audience may talk in language too advanced or too technical for them to understand and he usually goes on and on beyond the end of the lesson-time – a cardinal sin from the pupils' viewpoint. Interest in one's subject need not prevent a teacher from establishing a healthy rapport with his pupils so that he transmits on the correct wavelength for them to receive his signals; an intense teacher can become too serious to be effective. Now that geographical games have become a fashionable technique to employ, one wonders how successfully they can be played in school under the direction of a teacher whose natural pedagogical manner is severe and humourless? As long ago as 1817 the Abbé Gaultier wrote *A Complete Course of Geography by means of Instructive Games* and the rules he laid down in that book apply with equal force at the present time:

'The Instructor, while he teaches, must lay aside all magisterial authority, menaces and reprimands as incompatible with every idea of the game. Let him rather become the friend and companion of his pupils, cheerfully associating with them.'

Incidentally, one of the Abbé's games involved answering questions about places by using maps supplied for the purpose; the solution to the following example, relating to East Africa, would confound most teachers of geography at the present day!

Question: Which is bounded on the north by Monomugi, on the west by the Gulf of Sofala, on the south by Caffraria, and on the east by unknown regions?

(The answer is Monomotapa, which goes to show that there is nothing new in the recent spate of place-name changes in the African continent!)

However enthusiastic the teacher may be, he needs to preserve a sense of proportion and to develop an acute understanding of the capabilities of his class so that he can fit the level of discussion to their standard of acceptance. Apart from the warmth in his tone of voice, one means whereby a teacher can convey enjoyment of the subject is by introducing touches of humour to lighten the lesson. As a visual aid, the smile on a teacher's face can be just as effective as any coloured chart or projected picture.

Notice the irregular spacing of settlements on the map. This suggests that they originated many years BC, that is to say, before Christaller

(5) *The introduction of a little humour into the teaching situation can be hazardous but also rewarding, for its successful accomplishment is a measure of the teacher's rapport with the class.*

Although a sense of humour has often been quoted as a reliable attribute in a successful teacher, remarkably few books on education have attempted to analyse or discuss at length the functions, forms and social settings of classroom humour. Towards the end of the nineteenth century John Adams wrote a book on *The Herbartian Psychology Applied to Education* which is far more enjoyable to read than the title might suggest. In it he devoted a whole chapter to humour in teaching under the significant title 'A neglected educational organon'. Yet notwithstanding the attention which he directed towards it, comparatively little has been published on this topic until quite recently, so that for seventy years any references to humour in teaching tended to be few in number and slender in substance, either tucked away in pieces of psychological research into the characteristics of the good teacher or mentioned in manuals of instruction for those newly admitted to the profession. In 1931 R. B. Cattell submitted a questionnaire to about 500 persons comprising directors of education, inspectors, heads of primary and secondary schools and assistant teachers, inviting them to describe the ten most important features of a good young teacher and a good mature teacher. When the replies for these two categories were combined, a sense of humour emerged fifth out of twenty-two features, being preceded only by the traits of strong personality, intelligence, sympathy and fairness, although different groups of respondents varied in their estimation of the comparative importance of a sense of humour. Cattell also questioned a number of senior pupils and when these results were considered along with half a dozen independent researches by other investigators it appeared that pupils rated cheerfulness and a sense of humour as second only to kindness in their rank order of the qualities of a good teacher. In 1947 P. Witty analysed essays written by 12,000 high school students on the theme 'The teacher who has helped me most' and on this evidence a sense of humour was rated seventh out of twelve favourable characteristics. More recently, P. H. Taylor examined essays on 'A good teacher' written by more than 1,000 children in British primary and secondary schools, and concluded that pupils in secondary schools, especially the boys, were more appreciative than children in primary schools of a sense of humour in the teacher, this trait being rated more highly by the older pupils. A different approach was made by Frank Musgrove in his book *Patterns of Power and Authority in English Education* in which he devoted a whole chapter to the theme of 'Humour, sex and power'.

Hence it is true that for many years research into humour in school was usually reported in the form of unsubstantiated generalisations or as the coldly factual coded responses to tests and questionnaires. Direct observations of the uninhibited verbal exchanges between teacher and pupils in the course of ordinary lessons were rarely recorded or analysed. However, this latter type of investigation has recently been pursued by a number of educational sociologists whose findings are reported in books such as *Explorations in Classroom Observation* edited by Michael Stubbs and Sara Delamont and *School Experience: Explorations in the Sociology of Education* edited by Peter Woods and Martyn Hammersley. These revelations of the informal talk between teacher and pupils which is commonplace in many classrooms at the present time throw valuable light on the large amount of unimportant, inconsequential detail in these conversations as distinct from the solid subject-matter of the lesson. They also underline the important part played by humour in a diversity of forms.

Michael Finsbury, a lawyer in one of Robert Louis Stevenson's novels, attempted to cheer up his companion when they were both confronted with a serious problem by remarking that there is nothing like a little judicious levity. The ability to inject a light comment into the serious matter of schooling, or to appreciate the amusing side to an unforeseen situation which may arise suddenly during a lesson, creates a shared experience which brings together teacher and pupils for, as Gilbert Highet has suggested in his book *The Art of Teaching*, humour can act as a bridge between youth and maturity. Of course, young children may find amusement in simple sayings or situations which do not appear funny to the adult, while conversely the teacher may be highly amused by a slip of the tongue or spelling error which is committed unknowingly by a pupil in all seriousness; this is the essence of the howler which was considered at length in an earlier chapter. In effect, the appreciation of a joke is a measure of a person's breadth of knowledge and intellectual development, so that a story or incident may not amuse if the language or technical terms involved are not understood. John Adams illustrated this point with an example from *Punch* in which a young lady is in the company of two rival admirers. 'Do you like Botticelli' she asks one of them, who innocently replies 'N-no, I think I prefer Chianti'. Whereupon the other man whispers with malicious triumph into his rival's ear, 'Now you've done it. Botticelli isn't a wine, you idiot, it's a *cheese.*' In order to appreciate the humour of a situation it may also be necessary to know the shared experiences of a group, for certain comments will not be considered funny unless the history behind them is understood. A trite statement may be very amusing to the members of one household because it recalls for them the circumstances in which the same phrase was used many years earlier, and the incident is explained to a mystified onlooker as 'That saying has become a family joke in this house'. In like manner a visitor observing in a classroom may be puzzled by the laughter which accompanies a seemingly innocuous comment made by a pupil or a teacher. 'Strawberries' by Rob Walker and Clem Adelman contains a number of examples of this kind. A humorous remark or incident in the classroom can also assist the learner to remember a name, phrase or item of information for, as was indicated in an earlier chapter, the most effective mnemonics are often slightly amusing. In his novel about the classics master at Brookfield School who became known affectionately to the boys as 'Mr Chips', James Hilton derived some of his inspiration for this character from the example of his own father, who was for many years headmaster of an elementary school in a London suburb. The novelist described the transformation in Mr Chipping produced by his marriage to Katherine Bridges, a vivacious young governess with modern ideas. From being a shy, conscientious, reasonably capable and utterly uninspiring schoolmaster, who after twenty-five years of teaching was drifting into 'that creeping dry rot of pedagogy that is the worst and ultimate pitfall of the profession', he became under his wife's influence a more adventurous teacher whose discipline gained in strength by becoming less rigid. His lessons acquired some sparkle and he began to make little jokes, 'the sort that schoolboys like – mnemonics and puns that raised laughs and at the same time imprinted something in the mind'. One of his favourites was the Lex Canuleia, the law which allowed patricians to marry plebeians; after describing this to the form studying Roman history, he would add: 'So you see, if Miss Plebs wanted Mr Patrician to marry her, and he said he couldn't, she probably replied: "Oh yes you can, you liar!"'' When I first read this I was reminded of the anecdotes which used to enliven the Latin lessons during my own schooldays, especially the one about General Sir Charles Napier who was sent out to India to subdue the territory of Sind in 1843. Having successfully accomplished his mission he sent a cryptic dispatch from Hyderabad consisting of the single Latin word 'Peccavi', which means 'I have sinned'. (This anecdote clearly dates back to the days when all high-ranking officers in the British Army began their military training at an early age by learning to translate Caesar's *Gallic Wars*.)

In times past, when the schoolmaster ruled his class in an authoritarian manner and corporal punishment was common, any slight relaxation of the rigid control was welcomed by the pupils, so that any joke or humorous comment from the master was applauded loud and long for two very good reasons: it paid to please teacher by appearing to enjoy his jokes, however feeble they may have been, while the prolongation of the applause reduced the lesson-time available for the serious and dreadfully dull business of learning facts by heart. Oliver Goldsmith in his poem 'The Deserted Village' perceived the insincerity of much boyish laughter in class when the usually stern village schoolmaster was in a more relaxed mood:

> Full well they laughed with counterfeited glee
> At all his jokes, for many a joke had he.

The last half-dozen words imply that the schoolmaster had a well-defined stock of jokes which were only too familiar to the boys through a repetition of their telling. However, in recent years the atmosphere in many schools has become more relaxed, corporal punishment has almost disappeared, much of the drill, drudgery and memory work associated with learning has been abandoned, while the opportunities for light-hearted exchanges between teacher and pupils have increased. Nevertheless, many children who are not motivated to strive for success in examinations regard school as a boring waste of time and resentful scholars of low academic ability may consider laughter as a way of avoiding excessive boredom. In his chapter on 'Having a laugh: an antidote to schooling' Peter Woods describes the circumstances whereby laughter among children in class is a reaction against authority which can become a device for wasting time during school hours and may even appear subversive in intention. However, not all of the children of low ability in school are necessarily disgruntled and for the teacher of pupils such as these humour can be a means of direct social control as well as a way of initiating personal relationships with pupils. These topics are developed by Rob Walker and Ivor Goodson in their chapter on 'Humour in the classroom' in the book *School Experience* edited by Peter Woods and Martyn Hammersley. It is dangerous for a teacher to become too familiar with a class before he has got to know them well, and R. L. Bowley warns the young teacher against permitting laughter which is too loud, too long, too forced or too false. Derisive pupil laughter is a sign of indiscipline and a poor rapport between the teacher and his class; it approximates to insolence and when it breaks out a reversion to a more serious manner is perhaps the better course to be followed by the teacher, who needs to distinguish between situations when the class is laughing *with* him and when it is laughing *at* him. The latter circumstance may occur when the teacher makes some mistake, verbal or written, and the class laughs spontaneously at the error. The experienced teacher can laugh with them at himself, secure in the knowledge that his control is firm enough to permit a resumption of normal relations when the laughter has subsided; the newly qualified teacher is more likely to be embarrassed by his blunder, conscious of a temporary loss of prestige and accordingly he may issue peremptory orders to the class to resume their work. Michael Marland's recommendation in these circumstances is that if you do or say anything that inadvertently makes the children laugh *at* you, accept the situation rapidly and gracefully, for humourless indignation or pomposity will soon alienate the respect of a class.

A sense of humour by itself does not enable a teacher to maintain firm control over a class but when it is exercised judiciously it strengthens the understanding which has developed between the two sides. Experiment will enable the beginner to arrive at a style of presentation which is best suited to his particular talents and nature. One teacher may rely heavily upon the intonations of his voice, another on gestures with his hands, a third may preserve an impassive 'deadpan' countenance while describing an amusing incident, yet in their respective ways all can be equally successful in conveying a lighter touch to the proceedings. For the same reason humour should be handled with care by an inexperienced teacher until he has learned how to gauge the temper of the class. 'Don't smile before Christmas!' (or 'Never smile before Easter!', if you want to be ultra-cautious) are warnings to a probationary teacher that it is dangerous to be too jocular too rapidly. Notes which are supplied to students on teaching practice in a secondary school in South Yorkshire contain the following useful advice:

'A sense of humour is a valuable attribute but many young teachers use it too soon, too frequently, or with too little understanding of the sense of humour of children.'

A similar warning is issued by Frank Musgrove in his book on power and authority in education. Arguing that humour and sex can be equally dangerous to authority – which is why ruthlessly dedicated organisations like armies and monasteries have tended to be both single-sex and solemn – he suggests that the experienced teacher, recognising the potential threat of humour and sex, suppresses manifestations of both. Musgrove makes interesting observations on the contrasts between mixed and single-sex schools although he does not discuss whether girls are less appreciative than are boys of humour in the classroom.

In common with other teaching aids, humour is most effective if it is used in moderation; a surfeit of it is distracting and slightly sickening. Anecdotes are justified if they are relevant to the topic under consideration, otherwise they merely substitute one interest for another; used sparingly, however, they may provide illustrations which assist understanding of the main theme or they may capture the attention of the class at a moment when their interest is waning. During the war I heard of an unusual device to gain attention which was employed by a leading seaman whose duties involved giving formal instruction on a specific topic to each class of naval ratings in a training establishment. When the men had been marched by their class-leader into the lecture-room and were all seated the leading seaman instructor would enter the room, walk up the centre aisle to the blackboard, pick up a piece of chalk and proceed to draw a curved hat-peg in the top corner of the board. He then removed his cap, 'hung' it on the chalked peg – and to the astonishment of all the seated ratings, the cap remained there as if glued to the blackboard! Needless to say, that instructor had the rapt attention of every rating in the room before he had begun to address them, although whether he was able to retain their attention throughout the following ninety minutes depended on his skill as a teacher. The secret of his trick was that before the class had entered the lecture-room he had tapped a panel pin into the top corner of the blackboard. Around the pin, which was not visible from the front row of ratings, he then drew the peg with a piece of chalk and was able to hang his cap on the unseen pin.

(6) *There are occasions when it is useful for the teacher to be able to avoid creating laughter in class.*

Just as it is important for a teacher to deal with the subject-matter of the lesson at the level suited to the age and ability of the class, so too is it essential for him to appreciate the nature of the sense of humour in children in order to deal with it at the appropriate level when it is brought into action. Youngsters of primary school age delight in simple word-play and riddles which figure prominently in their verbal exchanges outside the classroom; I have already referred in an earlier chapter to the jingles and argot of the playground which form part of the subculture of school society. The book by Iona and Peter Opie is a storehouse of these juvenile conversation pieces, many of which (not being intended for adult ears) are vulgar and often anatomical. The teacher in the primary and secondary school has need to be aware of words and phrases which seem innocuous to the adult yet when uttered aloud can dispel the mental concentration of the class in a paroxysm of laughter. Some years ago an unnamed correspondent to the *Times Educational Supplement* offered some reflections upon commonplace words which have a dual meaning for children. For example, a 'drip', a 'dream', 'pop', 'sap' and 'rock' or the adjectives 'dim' and 'dumb' can create a ripple of amusement if used innocently by an unsuspecting teacher. Meat and potatoes are harmless foods to mention in class, but for some obscure reason the word 'sausage' has a humorous connotation, as does the mention of 'nuts'. The names of most animals leave children unmoved, but the monkey is a mirth-provoking mammal. The geography teacher should refer to groundnuts rather than peanuts or monkey nuts, if he wishes to keep the lesson on a serious footing, but he must expect a giggle or two at the first mention of dammed lakes, spits of land, or the river Po, just as the history teacher will raise a laugh when he first introduces a class to the Diet of Worms or the Rump

Parliament. References to parts of the anatomy between waist and knee must be chosen carefully if sniggering is to be avoided. Stomach, rear and posterior are received without emotion, but belly, bottom and backside are in a different category and if a rural scene in Palestine or Pakistan is being described it is preferable to refer to the peasant sitting on his donkey rather than on the three-letter synonym for that quadruped. A word which seems to amuse children of all ages is 'pants'; whenever it occurs as a verb or noun to indicate the hurried breathing which accompanies physical exertion, it is invariably interpreted by children as a reference to underwear. At their first encounter with Coleridge's poem *Kubla Khan* a class in English literature will listen in respectful silence to a reading of the opening seventeen lines, appreciating the sound of 'caverns measureless to man' and 'forests ancient as the hills', but when the next line is reached – 'As if this earth in fast thick pants were breathing' – the spell is broken, for the class is convulsed with laughter.

During a geography lesson reference may be made to places which have the power to raise a laugh or a giggle. An inoffensive name such as Stewart Island may cause a ripple of amusement if there happens to be a popular boy in the class whose name is Stewart. To the sport-loving youth in the 1970s, Romney Marsh was not merely associated with a breed of sheep and a low-lying area in Kent, for by changing one letter it created the name of a popular footballer. During the same decade Bulgaria and Orinoco acquired a new significance for children as the names of two characters in a group of singers who performed under the collective name of the Wombles. However it is important to realise that many popular entertainers and sporting personalities have the transient brilliance of meteors; they flash upon the canopy of public consciousness for a brief spell and are soon forgotten, so that a name which highly amuses one generation of children may be received without a flicker of emotion by a similar age-group a few years later. To regulate the serious tone of a lesson it is a distinct advantage if the teacher is familiar with the slang used by children and aware of their current idols in the world of sport and entertainment.

Changes which have taken place in the content of school geography have brought in their train modifications to the techniques employed in teaching it. In the days when pupils were expected to be docile recipients of information conveyed by their teachers the fashionable mode of instruction was to enforce the learning by heart of geographical locations and resources country by country and although Herbertson succeeded in simplifying and reducing the amount which children in school were required to learn, there was still heavy reliance upon memory work even if some of this could be reproduced in the form of sketch maps. In recent years, however, the teaching of geography has undergone a conceptual revolution and the current vogue is for problem-solving and hypothesis-testing to replace most of the rote memory work. This increase in the amount of activity and research by children has not reduced the task of the teacher – rather has it increased the preparatory work involved in assembling the materials for use in the classroom. Associated with the emergence of these new concepts and skills is a changed relationship between teacher and pupils, less formal than before, in which children are more vocal in expressing their opinions and preferences. In these altered conditions for learning there is ample scope for the introduction of minor matters and an element of humour in the teaching of geography.

REFERENCES

J. Adams, *The Herbartian Psychology applied to Education* (London, Heath, n.d.), ch. 8.

R. L. Bowley, *Teaching without Tears* (London, Centaur Press, 1961), pp. 28–9.

S. Butler, *Ernest Pontifex or the Way of All Flesh*, ed. D. F. Howard (London, Methuen, 1965), vol. 1, p. 98.

R. B. Cattell, 'The assessment of teaching ability', *British Journal of Educational Psychology*, vol. 1, 1931, pp. 48–71.

R. J. Chorley and P. Haggett (eds), *Frontiers in Geographical Teaching* (London, Methuen, 1965).

Department of Education and Science, *School Geography in the Changing Curriculum*, Education Survey No. 19 (London, HMSO, 1974).

C. B. Fawcett, 'On the teaching of the cycle of landforms', *Geographical Teacher* (now *Geography*), vol. 7, 1914, p. 26.

Daniel Fenning, *The Use of the Globes and the Rudiments of Geography*, 7th edn, rev. J. Moon (London, J. Johnson *et al.*, 1798).

A. Gaultier, *A Complete Course of Geography by means of Instructive Games* (London, Harris, 1817).

Martyn Hammersley and Peter Woods (eds), *The Process of Schooling, a Sociological Reader* (London, Routledge & Kegan Paul, 1976).

Gilbert Highet, *The Art of Teaching* (London, Methuen, 1951).

James Hilton, *Goodbye Mr Chips* (London, Hodder & Stoughton, 1934).

James Hilton, *To You, Mr Chips* (London, Hodder & Stoughton, 1938), ch. 1.

G. V. Jacks and R. O. Whyte, *The Rape of the Earth: A World Survey of Soil Erosion* (London, Faber, 1939), plate 45.

E. V. Lane, *South America* (London, Harrap, 1931).

H. J. Mackinder, 'Geography as a pivotal subject in education', *Geographical Journal*, vol. 57, 1921, p. 377.

Michael Marland, *The Craft of the Classroom* (London, Heinemann, 1975), p. 22.

Frank Musgrove, *Patterns of Power and Authority in English Education* (London, Methuen, 1971), ch. 4.

Robert Louis Stevenson, *The Wrong Box* (London, Chatto & Windus, 1911), p. 300.

Michael Stubbs and Sara Delamont (eds), *Explorations in Classroom Observation* (London, Wiley, 1976).

P. H. Taylor, 'Children's evaluations of the characteristics of the good teacher', *British Journal of Educational Psychology*, vol. 32, 1962, pp. 258–66.

Rob Walker and Clem Adelman, 'Strawberries', in M. Stubbs and S. Delamont (eds), op. cit., ch. 6.

Rob Walker and Ivor Goodson, 'Humour in the classroom', in *School Experience*, ed. Peter Woods and Martyn Hammersley (London, Croom Helm, 1977), ch. 8.

J. T. White, 'On being adaptable', in *New Movements in the Study and Teaching of Geography*, ed. N. J. Graves (London, Temple Smith, 1972), ch. 12.

P. Witty, 'An analysis of the personality traits of the effective teacher', *Journal of Educational Research*, vol. 30, 1947, pp. 662–71.

Peter Woods, 'Having a laugh: an antidote to schooling', in Martyn Hammersley and Peter Woods (eds), *op. cit.*, ch. 21.

Peter Woods and Martyn Hammersley (eds), *School Experience – Explorations in the Sociology of Education* (London, Croom Helm, 1977).

Bibliography

Adams, J., *The Herbartian Psychology Applied to Education* (London, Heath, n.d.).

Adams, J., *Errors in School* (London, University of London Press, 1927).

Baker, S. J., *The Australian Language* (Sydney, Currawong, 1966).

Balchin, W. G. V., 'The representation of true to scale linear values on map projections', *Geography*, vol. 36, 1951, pp. 120−4.

Benstead, C. R., *The Weather Eye* (London, Robert Hale, 1940).

Bibby, C., *The Art of the Limerick* (London, The Research Publishing Co., 1978).

Bowley, R. L., *Teaching without Tears* (London, Centaur Press, 1961).

Cattell, R. B., 'The assessment of teaching ability', *British Journal of Educational Psychology*, vol. 1, 1931, pp. 48−71.

Chorley, R. J., and Haggett, P. (eds), *Frontiers in Geographical Teaching* (London, Methuen, 1965).

Coates, B. (ed.), *Census Atlas of South Yorkshire* (Sheffield University, Department of Geography, 1974).

Cole, J. P., and Beynon, N. J., *New Ways in Geography*, Book 2 (Oxford, Blackwell, 1973).

Darby, H. C., 'The problem of geographical description', *Transactions of the Institute of British Geographers*, 1962, pp. 1−14.

Darby, H. C. (ed.), *A New Historical Geography of England* (Cambridge, Cambridge University Press, 1973).

Department of Education and Science, *School Geography in the Changing Curriculum*, Education Survey No. 19 (London, HMSO, 1974).

Disley, J., *Your Way with Map and Compass* (London, Blond Educational, 1971).

Fairgrieve, J., *Geography in School* (London, University of London Press, 1926).

Fleming, P., *Brazilian Adventure* (London, Odyssey Library, 1966).

Gatty, H., *Nature Is Your Guide* (London, Collins, 1958).

Gaultier, A., *A Complete Course of Geography by means of Instructive Games* (London, Harris, 1817).

Gelling, M., *Signposts to the Past: Place-Names and the History of England* (London, Dent, 1978).

Gould, P., and White, R., *Mental Maps* (Harmondsworth, Penguin, 1974).

Hammersley, M., and Woods, P. (eds), *The Process of Schooling, a Sociological Reader*, (London, Routledge & Kegan Paul, 1976).

Highet, G., *The Art of Teaching* (London, Methuen, 1951).

Hilton, J., *Goodbye Mr Chips* (London, Hodder & Stoughton, 1934).

Hilton, J., *To You, Mr Chips* (London, Hodder & Stoughton, 1938).

Inwards, R., *Weather Lore*, ed. and rev. E. L. Hawke (London, Rider & Co. for the Royal Meteorological Society, 1950).

Ishida, R. (ed.), *Understanding Japan*, Bulletin No. 1 of the International Society for Educational Information (Tokyo, ISEI, 1960).

Jahoda, G., 'The development of children's ideas about country and nationality', *British Journal of Educational Psychology*, vol. 33, 1963, pp. 47−60.

Keltie, J. S., 'Geographical education', *Royal Geographical Society Supplementary Papers*, vol. 1, 1886, pp. 447–594.

Kimmins, C. W., *The Springs of Laughter* (London, Methuen, 1928).

King, G. E. (ed.), *Conflict and Harmony: A Source-Book of Man in his Environment* (London, George Philip, 1972).

Mackinder, H. J., 'Geography as a pivotal subject in education', *Geographical Journal*, vol. 57, 1921, pp. 376–84.

Manley, G., *Climate and the British Scene* (London, Collins, 1952).

Marland, M., *The Craft of the Classroom* (London, Heinemann, 1975).

Matthews, C. M., *Place Names of the English-Speaking World* (London, Weidenfeld & Nicolson, 1972).

Mill, H. R., *The Record of the Royal Geographical Society 1830–1930* (London, Royal Geographical Society, 1930).

Milner, D., *Children and Race* (Harmondsworth, Penguin, 1975).

Moorhouse, G., *Britain in the Sixties: The Other England* (Harmondsworth, Penguin, 1964).

Musgrove, F., *Patterns of Power and Authority in English Education*, (London, Methuen, 1971).

Opie, I., and P., *The Lore and Language of Schoolchildren* (London, Oxford University Press, 1959).

Orwell, G., 'Boys' weeklies', in *The Collected Essays, Journalism and Letters of George Orwell*, ed. S. Orwell and I. Angus (London, Secker & Warburg, 1968), pp. 460–84.

Orwell, G., *The Road to Wigan Pier* (London, Gollancz, 1937).

Pocock, D. C. D., 'The novelist's image of the north', *Transactions of the Institute of British Geographers* (new series), vol. 4, 1979, pp. 62–76.

Ross, A. S. C., *How to Pronounce It*, (London, Hamish Hamilton, 1970).

Sellar, W. C., and Yeatman, R. J., *1066 and All That* (London, Methuen, 1930).

Sellar, W. C., and Yeatman, R. J., *And Now All This* (London, Methuen, 1932).

Stewart, G. R., *Names on the Land* (New York, Random House, 1945).

Stubbs, M., and Delamont, S. (eds), *Explorations in Classroom Observation* (London, Wiley, 1976).

Taylor, P. H., 'Children's evaluations of the characteristics of the good teacher', *British Journal of Educational Psychology*, vol. 32, 1962, pp. 258–66.

Trovato, B., *Best Howlers* (London, Wolfe Publishing, 1970).

Vernon, P., *The Certificate of Secondary Education: An Introduction to Objective-Type Examinations*, SSEC Examinations Bulletin No. 4 (London, HMSO, 1964).

White, J. T., 'On being adaptable', in *New Movements in the Study and Teaching of Geography*, ed. N. J. Graves (London, Temple Smith, 1972), ch. 12.

Witty, P., 'An analysis of the personality traits of the effective teacher', *Journal of Educational Research*, vol. 30, 1947, pp. 662–71.

Woods, P., and Hammersley, M. (eds), *School Experience – Explorations in the Sociology of Education* (London, Croom Helm, 1977).

Index